Together by Design

Together by Design

—

THE ART AND ARCHITECTURE OF COMMUNAL LIVING

William Richards

PRINCETON ARCHITECTURAL PRESS · NEW YORK

For Margot, made during her first year

Published by
Princeton Architectural Press
70 West 36th Street
New York, NY 10018
www.papress.com

ISBN 978-1-64896-027-7

Production editor: Kristen Hewitt
Design concept: Paula Baver / Typesetting: Benjamin English
Cover design: Paul Wagner

Library of Congress Control Number: 2021952804

Contents

Introduction: Living Together

We are all learning how to live with one another in new and different ways at the intersection of political upheaval and pandemic malaise. Partisanship has long outstripped probity in government, and a rampant virus and its variants have taken millions of lives. The legacy of climate inaction continues to threaten our planet, and its related crises have revealed the depths of economic disenfranchisement. How we choose to live and the communities we call home are the front lines of any national crisis defined by mind-bendingly huge figures. Last year, more than half a million Americans were counted as homeless—a figure that experts believe is lower than actual numbers and one that had been rising even before COVID-19. A 2020 Aspen Institute article revealed that thirty million to forty million Americans reported they had no or only slight confidence they could pay the following month's rent and were therefore deemed at risk of eviction, with or without a moratorium. Even after the first waves of pandemic-induced joblessness subsided, rent debt to landlords plagued more than seven million Americans in 2021, according to the US Census Bureau. The rise of housing insecurity exacerbated a simmering crisis of financial insecurity that had been deepening amid record-high stock prices. Food deserts also remain problematic in light of what some researchers call a global syndemic (or synergistic epidemic of linked health problems)—namely, obesity, undernutrition, and climate change. The United Nations System Standing Committee on Nutrition reported in 2020 that the number of communities without access to affordable and healthy food has been declining, but more than eighteen million Americans still live in "low-access" census tracts. The report also notes that compared to white Americans, 30 percent more Americans of color live in food deserts.

How we choose to live and the communities we call home might reflect these and other grim statistics, but they might also proffer solutions on the front lines of our everyday lives— in communities themselves. This is a book about the intention of individuals to act as a community and how the values of cohousing and co-living communities can create solutions-oriented structures of mutual support. It is also about how specific communities have addressed such challenges as climate action by living in sustainable ways amid environmental threats; aging with dignity and independence in a society that assumes old is defined by infirmities and helplessness; and finding a balance between sociability and privacy in a digital world that seems to imperil both.

This book features projects that address questions about communal living and communal space. It deals with the relationship between architects and communities, and between their shared goals and respective needs. It also provides context for the explosion of recent press coverage on intentional communities, which might very well signal the movement's coming of age, such as Nathan Heller's 2021 *New Yorker* article on intentional living, which places it in the context of mostly millennials who enmesh their lives (and living spaces) with strangers. The world of intentional communities is far more diverse than this, and there are useful distinctions to make between cohousing, co-living, and cooperatives, just as there are useful distinctions to be made between the economic choices of third-age pensioners in London and the associative choices of LGBTQ seniors in Durham, North Carolina. Heller writes that "punctilious types" distinguish between cohousing, co-living, and cooperatives, but these are more than distinctions. They are fundamental choices that residents must make about self-governance in determining how their daily lives will play out and the kinds of people their self-selected communities will attract.

Even before COVID-19 forced many people to reevaluate their living environments, there had been a groundswell of interest in the kinds of choices that co-living represents, covered by outlets from the *New York Times* to the *Los Angeles Times* to *Christianity Today*. As an outgrowth of the overworked "tiny house" coverage, shelter magazines turned to co-living and cohousing projects over the last decade as new evidence that alternative living principles were more popular (and agreeable) than once thought. McKinney York Architects has designed two "micro homes" for Community First!, a supportive community for people emerging from chronic homelessness in Austin, Texas. The firm's designs were covered by *Dwell* and contribute to what can only be called a village of two-hundred-square-foot cottages arranged on a site to engender collectivism while also securing a sense of individuation. Here the phrase *living together* applies faintly to lots of adjacent tiny homes, and for this community to exist, hundreds of people have to choose to live together.

Still, most of the attention lately has been on the millennial- and xennial-centric communities that have grown in the wake of urban gentrification. Los Angeles's Treehouse Hollywood (also profiled by Heller) is a forty-thousand-square-foot community that attracts "neo-homesteaders," in a nod to good old American self-determination and western migration 130 years ago, to its site in the shadow of the 101 freeway and blocks from Hollywood and Vine. Like other co-living communities, Treehouse Hollywood represents concentric circles of private and public space, where personal choices and communal interests blend together to define its particular ethos. Smaller and less expensive "flats" and larger, more expensive "studios" define the inner circle for residents, and common areas, including kitchens and a music studio, define the outer circle. At the expense of being punctilious, the project is a good example of co-living in a twenty-first-century twist on what used to be called a group house: amenities here are not cobbled together by a few strangers renting a row house but are abundant and available in a highly curated way. Flash aside, Treehouse Hollywood is a lifestyle and not just an address. It reflects economic and social choices by its residents, who wish to associate their identities with their environments and

Like other co-living communities, Treehouse Hollywood in Los Angeles
represents concentric circles of private and public spaces, where personal
choices and communal interests blend to define its ethos.

The Nordic Pavilion at the 2021 Venice Architecture Biennale hosted
What We Share: A Model for Cohousing, a communal-living
installation designed by Helen & Hard to demonstrate how semiprivate
subzones facilitate group activity and personal respite.

vice versa—not unlike the nuclear family of four in a suburban ranch-style house, or a dual-income/no-kids couple living
in a Miami high-rise. Even though the US Census Bureau has
tallied a record-high thirty-six million Americans living alone
today, it is still only 28 percent of the population. Most people always will live with at least one other person (and usually more)—meaning that living together remains the order
of the day.

Hashim Sarkis, the architect and curator of the 2021
Venice Architecture Biennale, took the vicissitudes of living
together as his theme, conjuring myriad answers from design
teams around the world. The Nordic Pavilion hosted the
Norwegian firm Helen & Hard (designers of the award-
winning co-living project Vindmøllebakken, completed in
2019 in Stavanger, Norway) to ask "What are you willing to
share?" as the idea behind their proposal for communal living and what they call semi-private sub-zones. Their contri-
bution was well crafted, replete with beautifully milled spruce
surfaces left unvarnished and carefully placed pops of color
throughout the exhibit. Visitors could pretend to be the residents and circulate around the mocked-up space in faint rev-
erie over the communal living ideal. They could also watch
videos positioned strategically throughout the space to tell
a fuller story about nineteenth-century worker collectives
in France, seventeenth-century walled villages in southern
China, and, of course, Nordic cohousing from the 1960s on.
Even if living together in a purposeful way is not a new idea,
as one video attested, it is an enduring ideal—and Helen &

Hard's installation was the product of a participatory process with Vindmøllebakken residents, which means it might not have been the ideal community for everyone in the world, but it did reflect the ideal for one group of Norwegians at a moment and place in time.

Most of the Biennale news coverage vaulted past sober responses to the theme of living together in new ways and focused squarely on what the design media claimed was the curatorial capriciousness of Sarkis's "favourite candy" at a time when resources might have been better spent elsewhere instead of funding a business-as-usual exhibition with a large carbon footprint in an ecologically imperiled city barely three feet above sea level. "What is certain is that the post-pandemic experience and these accurate critiques show the end of an era," wrote Roberto Zancan in *Domus* (May 26, 2021). "The *Trente Glorieuses* (1990–2020) are over," he said, "and we are witnessing the end of a cycle." Whether or not this era has ended with a bang or a whimper, the new baseline of understanding that the status quo is no longer working is a fitting rejoinder to the claim that intentional communities (and cohousing and co-living) have always represented a critique of accepted norms.

The coverage of the Venice Architecture Biennale generally, and the decade-long increase in coverage of cohousing specifically, is necessary reading to make sense of how COVID-19 has altered the rites and rituals of our lives, from graduation ceremonies and café culture to baseball games, Sunday services, and visits to the public library. As we deal with the ongoing pandemic, the bungled response by certain governments at critical times, and our shared hope for recovery, questions centered on how we live, work, learn, and socialize together continue to be under the microscope—in terms of both communicable pathogens that threaten us all and new realizations about what we are willing to tolerate. Cohousing, co-living, and intentional communities are new and nothing new at the same time, but these models of livability suggest that solutions to some of the biggest economic and health challenges are within our grasp so long as we perpetuate the ideals of community writ large, and embrace our actual communities just outside our doors.

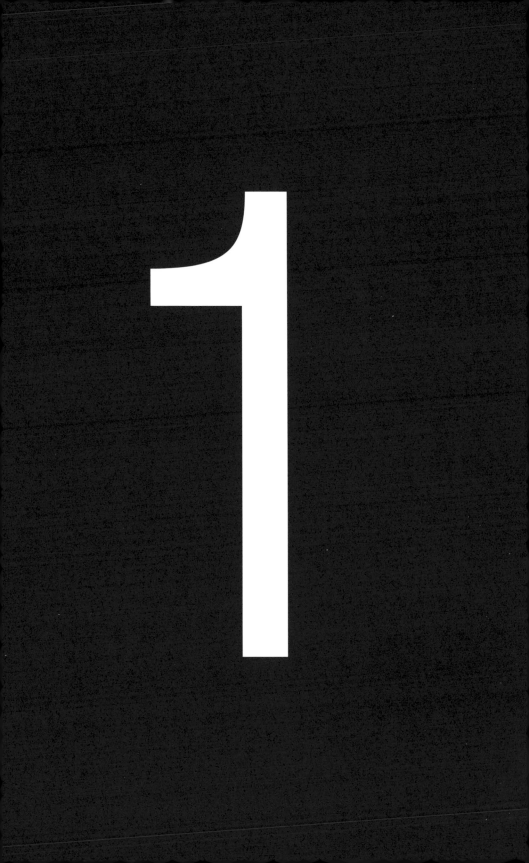

1

Intention and Architecture

ARCHITECTURE HAS ALWAYS PROVIDED A VESSEL FOR individuals and communities to live their beliefs, and when it is designed for intentional communities, it reflects the social structures their members determine to be productive and supportive. Intention defines nearly every aspect of architecture, from a building's orientation to the sun and arrangement of spaces according to a program to the precise square footage. It can be a matter of custom, such as the building traditions of cathedrals, meetinghouses, mosques, or synagogues, which

Frontispiece of abbé Marc-Antoine Laugier's 1775 *Essai sur l'architecture* (2nd ed.) by Charles Dominique Joseph Eisen and engraved by Jacques Aliamet. Laugier's allegory of the primitive hut, introduced by Vitruvius, signals an evolution from building to intentional architecture and, therefore, to a theoretical foundation for all architects.

reflect congregational requirements for hierarchies and liturgies. It can be a matter of civility, such as roadways, police stations, or town halls, which reflect a community's requirements for safety and governance. It can be a matter of law, such as zoning and permits, which require architects to design precisely and contractors to build squarely.

The Vitruvian primitive hut venerated by the abbé Marc-Antoine Laugier and published in his 1755 *Essai sur l'architecture* is an ideal form that gives shelter to its inhabitants and gives purpose to architecture itself. Shelter sought by individuals, their families, and their communities is the foundation on which other intentional forms of architecture can evolve, from the cellar to the basilica, or from the Circus Maximus to Lambeau Field. Laugier's hut signals an evolution from building to intentional architecture. When individuals recognize their commitment to each other, they enshrine their shared intentions in communities.

The architectural response to the concept of community is much broader than simply "housing" as it has been defined in the most basic sense of shelter. The word *housing* has long signified public housing, ennobled by good intentions, but tarnished by the ways in which economics, structural racism, and failed place-making have converged. The Reagan-era "war on drugs" was fought in public-housing communities, and the resulting incarceration and recidivism rates have plagued African American communities for two generations. The absenteeism among African American men aged twenty-five to fifty-four from their demographic cohort has forced mothers, grandmothers, grandfathers, siblings, and cousins to be proxies for father figures. This has had a direct impact on the composition of African American households in the United States and therefore on how two generations of Americans have considered and reconsidered what normative living conditions could mean.

Another architectural response to the concept of community has been to optimize space based on the functional movements and habits of its user groups. Among the transformations between the Victorian era of architecture and the modern era of architecture is a shift away from dedicated and discrete spaces toward multipurpose and flexible spaces, whenever possible, in homes, schools, university dormitories, offices, libraries, and municipal buildings, among other types. In conversations with clients, architects are routinely intentional about balancing communal and personal functions, public and private spaces, and group needs in light of individual requirements. Whether they are designing a marching band's rehearsal space or a legislative chamber, architects accommodate knowable users, as represented by the client, who move in on opening day, as well as unknowable users, generations hence, who will become stewards of those spaces, routines, customs, and communities. Laugier's hut is still the foundation, as all architecture is a home for something and groups of somebodies.

The nearest beneficiary of Laugier's hut is the concept of the home, itself theorized and historicized repeatedly as the most important reflection of a society's values, not to mention individual expression (in light of or in rebellion against probity), architectural experimentation in materiality and form, and the symbols and accoutrements of status. Home is one's castle, home is where the heart is, there is no place like home, charity begins at home, the home stretch, come home to roost, home for the holidays, bring home the bacon, and no direction home—ceaseless idioms in a quantity unmatched by other places we spend time at like the grocery store, the car wash, or the library.

The homeownership rate in the United States is about 67 percent at the time of this writing, which suggests that the American dream is alive and well for about two-thirds of the population. Hyperbole aside, what the homeownership rate actually suggests is a nation of unaffiliated citizens who own an average of twenty-six hundred square feet of interior space. Maybe they chat with one another over the fence of their average quarter acre of land or in the mailroom of their twelve-story high-rise. But, by and large, Americans live separate lives that are calibrated to ensure privacy and designed to create physical borders that enforce social boundaries. This is the mainstream, and, by definition, any other attitude toward privacy, community, space, and place is considered an alternative to this mainstream. Cohousing is an alternative representing intentional and community-minded individuals who are unaffiliated in the familial sense but arguably closer with one another than they are with their own blood relatives. The Cohousing Association of America tracks nearly two hundred cohousing communities in the United States. Globally, that number is much higher, with more examples in every European country (including cohousing's origin, Denmark, where an estimated seven hundred communities have formed since the early 1990s), as well as Australia, Canada, China, and New Zealand.

Over the past five years, intentional communities have been featured in national weeklies such as the *Atlantic*, *Forbes*, *Time* magazine, and trade publications like *Multifamily Executive* as evidence of co-living, communal living, and cohousing—terms that are sometimes commingled but ought not to be for reasons that are discussed in this book. The media coverage of intentional communities has been fairly uniform, invariably noting that more Americans are living in "unconventional" ways beyond the normative standards we ascribe to nuclear family life or cohabitation. There are precedents for this new trend, whether it is a medieval guild or heritage-based veneration for elders or hippie communes. Of course, deep down (and for economic, social, or familial reasons), we have always been pack animals who band together and prefer to live together, despite the so-called virtues of individuation and self-actualization in twentieth-century psychology.

In other words, we are not innately solitary creatures, but modernity has made us this way. There is evidence and commentary for at least a century about this shift away from communal living to self-selecting isolation, and back again. Essays like Georg Simmel's "The Metropolis and Mental Life" (1903) profoundly influenced how urbanists and architects thought about the paradox of psychological isolation occurring even in the middle of a city full of people. The Chicago school of sociology was founded on industrialization's perceived ills and its effect on social structures, and is aligned in spirit with William Morris, John Ruskin, and A. W. N. Pugin's Arts and Crafts mission to (among other commercial aims) raise the standards of design eroded by machine reproduction. Urban geographers in the 1960s and 1970s creatively addressed the class and economic implications of how we live among one another at a time when architects gathered ideas from anthropology, economics, psychology, and sociology to forge a human-centric approach to design that presaged what we call public-interest design today.

Despite these critical inquiries into sameness for nearly a century, there was money to be made in architecture and the broader construction industry at midcentury in designing for the status quo, as symbolized by the various Levittowns along the East Coast—the very definition of a mainstream and conventional housing ideal, or "little boxes made of ticky tacky," to quote the songwriter Malvina Reynolds. In his 1967 study *The Levittowners*, Herbert Gans noted Levittown's three chief shortcomings. First, its residents could not cope with conflict whatsoever among neighbors. Second, they could not deal with diversity of lifestyles (what he called pluralism), and they could not tolerate what they considered the intrusion of public services like bus routes into their communities. The physical neighborhood, in other words, was supposed to be an archipelago of homeowners, each in possession of their own respective islands. "The third shortcoming of the community,"

Herbert Gans's *Levittowners: Ways of Life and Politics in a New Suburban Community* focuses on one of the three recognized Levittown communities, which was developed in Willingboro Township, New Jersey, beginning in 1958, the same year that the second in Levittown, Pennsylvania, was completed. This photograph was taken in 1959 after the first wave of families moved into the latter.

wrote Gans, "is the failure to establish a meaningful relationship between home and community." In this way, he believed, "Levittown is America."

Today, the strains of sameness still define the dominant cultures of our globalized, politically antagonistic, and economically divided time, but increasingly potent arguments about diversity and inclusion heighten our awareness of how we choose to live, what our choices mean, and why we participate in (or are attracted to) certain lifestyles. Going back to contemporary coverage of cohousing in the media, we are also beginning to see deeper and more responsible coverage of the cultural, economic, and racial dimensions of how we live—either by choice or by circumstance. Extended families or adopted families are major plotlines in everything from *Sesame Street* and procedural dramas to mockumentaries and Lifetime holiday romances. In 2021, Target sold coffee mugs emblazoned with "Ask me about my pronouns." Private-sector employers from Wall Street to Main Street see flexible working arrangements for their legion of employees, whose circumstances are not homogeneous, as an asset to profitability rather than a threat.

Architects widely reject sameness in their client discovery and design processes in favor of accommodating user groups in a meaningful way while creating value for their clients. In architectural circles, aging in place and multigenerational housing reflect increased awareness of the benefits of (and reasons for) living together in more communal ways that predate *The Brady Bunch* or *The Adventures of Ozzie and Harriet* model

With new construction that sits on the ruins of a once-viable retail space that had fallen on hard times, buildings like The Shay in Washington, DC, attempt to soften downtown living for twenty-something transplants.

In adaptive-reuse projects gutted to the shell, buildings like Atlantic Plumbing Residences by Morris Adjmi Architects, also in Washington, DC, evoke a sense of place with a nod to a commercial past (however feeble that nod ends up being through photomurals, signage, or iconography).

of probity or normalcy. New apartment communities (formerly known as just "apartments") have crested on the wave of gentrification in every major American city to drive structural economic change. With new construction that sits on the ruins of once-viable retail that had fallen on hard times, buildings like The Shay in Washington, DC, for instance, attempt to soften downtown living for twenty-something transplants with a "sparkling" pool and "spacious" media lounge, not to mention "plush seating" on the landscaped rooftop. In adaptive-use projects gutted to the shell, buildings like Atlantic Plumbing, also in Washington, DC, evoke a sense of place with a nod to a commercial past (however feeble it might be).

Atlantic Plumbing's features and amenities are nearly identical to The Shay's, although the former is more explicit in advertising rooftop living rooms (plural) with "grills and kitchenettes" just off the "expansive" sundeck and rooftop pool. In either building, and in nearly all cases for buildings like them, the atmosphere is one of an adult dormitory for a fifth or sixth year of college, a formative experience that seems to be deeply embedded in the psyche of Americans seeking to define young adulthood. But the parity between dorm life and postdorm life is not new either. In "College Students Live Here," a 1961 study of community and living trends on campuses published by the Educational Facilities Laboratory, researchers noted something that could very well describe apartment communities like The Shay or Atlantic Plumbing.

"The coming decade will see smaller living units combined within larger structures. Housing projects on the whole

In "College Students Live Here," a 1961 study of community and living
trends on campuses, researchers presaged some of the qualities
that could very well describe today's adult dormitories: smaller individual
living units, more shared amenities, and self-contained facilities.

will be self-contained, each with its own facilities for cultural activities, indoor and outdoor recreation, and dining," wrote Harold Riker, chief author of the study. "Commons rooms will shrink in size and expand in number. The formal lobby and lounge will yield space to smaller, more casual rooms that can be used for study and discussion as well as entertaining and recreation."

Why are projects like The Shay or Atlantic Plumbing or hundreds like them significant? While they host a largely single and transient population in studios and one- and two-bedroom units, they go to great strides to create a communal set of amenities that encourages living beyond the walls of one's apartment. This is a distinct shift away from apartments or dormitories two generations ago, which had limited communal space to a laundry facility or a lobby with mailboxes. Only the largest prewar and postwar apartment complexes included mini-marts for last-minute bottles of overpriced wine and dusty snacks. Today, there are saunas, massage rooms, game rooms, restaurants, bars, roof decks, barbecue pits, small and large event spaces for rent, and even guest suites for out-of-town visitors. Most of the time, these buildings incorporate retail space at ground level—Warby Parker, Sweetgreens, and Starbucks an elevator ride away. Unlike cohousing, these are considered co-living communities of unaffiliated individuals living together by choice, but not necessarily for any ideological, religious, or social motives. Semantics are important between cohousing and co-living. These co-living communities are simply shortened to "communities" in the parlance of rental market advertising and value propositions. In the spirit of the precision of intentional communities, it is worthwhile to be precise about the subsets that define them.

DEFINITIONS AND VARIANTS
OF INTENTIONAL COMMUNITIES

All cohousing projects are intentional communities, but not all intentional communities are cohousing projects. Co-living means a community of unaffiliated individuals renting in a nonownership position who seek out and utilize shared amenities designed to facilitate sociability. Co-living means the apartment communities just discussed do not necessarily encourage transience, but they are also not designed to be practical, long-term living situations for people who customarily and eventually make life choices that require more space, more privacy, or both. In short, co-living means that there is a stated interest in living with others among residents who must abide by general rules of acceptable behavior, but not necessarily on the basis of belief, interest, or value.

Cohousing, in contrast, is a long-term arrangement for affiliated individuals in alignment on beliefs, interests, and values; who regularly share meals, responsibilities, resources, and their own time; and who are committed to decision-making processes aimed at balancing individual ideas in service to the greater good of the community. On a scale of intensity, cohousing is a more intentional kind community than co-living, which is represented by established communities, such as Arcosanti (Arizona), Findhorn (Scotland), or Village

Hearth (North Carolina), and which have an explicit communal purpose, such as self-sustaining urbanism, ecology, life stage, identity, or inclusiveness.

There are other types of intentional communities that fall outside the co-living and cohousing subsets discussed in this book. Some are built on a shared outlook, such as the doomsday prepper communities Trident Lakes in Texas or Fortitude Ranch in Colorado, which are about future proofing against societal breakdown. Some are patchworks of privately owned properties and like-minded neighbors in gated communities whose residents are governed by legally binding covenants. Others offer private ownership within a larger piece of property, requiring an application for membership and formal acceptance by something resembling a cooperative board. Dormitories also offer a rich discussion about intentionality and the responsibility of in loco parentis held by schools, whether ivy and stone residential quads on the British model at places like Princeton University or the rustic hilltop village of Eero Saarinen's Morse and Ezra Stiles Residential Colleges at Yale University. So-called retirement communities fit nicely here with regard to intentionality, and like the amenity-filled co-living apartments, they, too, are competing for residents. But this is where the lines begin to blur, as senior living is moving beyond co-living and gaining ground as a popular subset of cohousing, examples of which are explored in this book under the more inclusive term *third-age housing*.

There are three basic dimensions to cohousing as it is practiced today. First, its philosophy is broadly based in consensus and cooperation, and interpreted through the interests of a group whose members do not just live next to one another but choose to live among one another. This approach remains outside the mainstream of the way most people choose to structure their lives. It also remains outside the mainstream of banking and zoning. "What do banks care about more than anything else? Risk," says the architect Charles Durrett; he and the development consultant Kathryn McCamant are considered the progenitors of the American cohousing movement and have, together and apart, designed or advised the residents of dozens of cohousing projects in the last forty years.

"So, if we bring future residents to the table and they all have letters saying they qualify for a loan, their risk goes down, so banks like us for our projects," says Durrett. "We don't start construction until we have 75 percent of the residents, and that's another plus for the bank. What's not normal for the banks, however, is that the word *cohousing* doesn't show up once [in their forms]. We have to make 'condos.'"

Over the years, financing for cohousing community members has been accomplished by structuring the project like privately owned condominiums or creating limited-equity cooperative housing. Communities may also be entirely owned by nonprofit associations, to which residents pay "rent." Still others combine various approaches to financing and ownership. One particularly involved model is the Low Impact Living Affordable Community (LILAC), a limited development of twenty homes in Leeds, England, that stands in an area where the median disposable household income is £29,000 (or about $38,500), just a shade off the national median disposable income of £29,400 (or about $39,100). Its ownership model is unique among many cohousing communities of its kind as a Mutual Home Ownership Society (MHOS), which means that the society holds the mortgage and members of the society—the residents—hold leases and pay an equity share to the society while retaining an equity position, and these shares cover the mortgage held by the society after maintenance and insurance deductions. Residents pay 35 percent of their disposable income each month, up from the national average of 17.7 percent per month among individual owner-occupiers and 32.8 percent among renters. When LILAC residents move away, their equity shares are put up for sale. If LILAC residents lose their jobs temporarily or their income drastically changes, their payments are adjusted, still keeping at 35 percent of net. To date, three communities in England have adopted this model—LILAC, Terrace 21 in Liverpool, and Harbour Community in Stroud—and a fourth in York is in the early stages of adopting it.

Financing and ownership aside, questions about zoning in the United States inevitably come up for architects and their clients in planning and developing a cohousing community. Ironically, cohousing communities are usually designated planned unit developments (PUDs) of completely self-contained subdivisions, which made places like Levittown and suburban sprawl possible in the post–World War II era. Some municipalities do not allow for PUDs, while others are caught between adapting outmoded zoning designations to accommodate new types of development and implementing form-based zoning codes aimed at creating common standards and predictable results around environmental conservation, historic preservation, or some other interest based in the commonwealth.

Even if these hurdles present challenges for architects and their clients, cohousing continues to draw the interest of new generations of residents. As recently as 2018, the Cohousing Association of America counted more than 166 cohousing communities in the United States and another seventeen under construction. Remarkably and perhaps a little incredibly, there were an additional 144 in the planning stage at that time, effectively doubling the number of community groups that had, at least, signaled their collective intention to build and, among the earliest communities, were enjoying several active decades in the cohousing lifestyle. The first widely recognized cohousing community in the United States, Muir Commons (designed by Durrett and McCamant and completed in 1991) remains viable as a stable, affordable community with low turnover. Durrett notes that among the initial twenty-five homes at Muir Commons, twenty-three were purchased by first-time homebuyers, some of whom have stayed decades. "I go there a lot since it's fifty miles from me, and it's surprising to me how many people still live there," says Durrett. "The first resident at Muir Commons didn't move away for twelve years. We did twenty-five houses and it took twelve years, which makes their mobility half of the typical American's mobility, because the typical American moves every six years. Since nobody wanted to move, they hired me to do additions because they had kids."

Cohousing also continues to grow in terms of the different kinds of interests represented by groups. The Foundation for Intentional Community lists ecovillages, communes, student co-ops, Jewish communities, and Christian communities in its taxonomy of intentional-living terms that have cohousing overlays. The UK Cohousing Network lists twelve major types of cohousing projects: senior, intergenerational, LGBTQ, vegan, vegetarian, ecological, community land trust (CLT), co-operative, new construction (or new build), self-build, retrofit, and refurbished. While this type of diversity drives the interests of residents, there are some optimal conditions under which cohousing communities tend to thrive. One is the size of the community, with an ideal range between twenty-something and thirty-something in the numbers of residents, which is generally echoed by architects working in this arena. "There seems to be consensus that twenty or thirty is the sweet spot for numbers of residents, to try and create community accountability and dynamic. Bigger than that, decision-making becomes more difficult. Smaller, and one personality might dominate," says Patrick Devlin, an architect and partner at London's Pollard Thomas Edwards (PTE) who specializes in third-age cohousing.

Another dimension of cohousing is its site plan and scale, which facilitates group dynamics and defines an architectural philosophy of cohousing based on a village model. Cohousing residences are designed to find efficiencies through a limited

The Low-Impact Living Affordable Community (LILAC), a limited development of twenty homes in Leeds, England, has a unique ownership model among many cohousing communities of its kind, but its fundamentals of balancing private and public spheres are standard among cohousing projects.

menu of layouts; typically, they are conjoined with party walls into larger host structures that open onto common green areas, patios, and walkways. Almost always, these communities have a central hub called a common house, a communal house, a central house, or something similar where the community's intentions to live together according to precepts of cohousing play out daily. Along the streetscapes, one- to two-story and even sometimes three-story structures are ideal for cohousing communities in relation to the human scale, which maps onto what some architects believe to be a kind of golden ratio for the walkable streetscape as outlined by various groups over the years, including the Congress for the New Urbanism (CNU), the New Urban Guild, and the Council for European Urbanism. Porches are ubiquitous as liminal spaces of both conviviality and quiet contemplation—spaces that can be invitational or noninvitational. Some communities integrate parking close to individual residences, particularly if mobility and access is a priority. Others relegate parking to a far corner or marginalize it in favor of a more walkable community. Some have a communal workshop, a fitness room, a garden, or an art studio, but many have all four in addition to the multipurpose common house.

There are also some common but less obvious design elements that facilitate group dynamics, chiefly the ways in which public and private lives can unfold on a spectrum and in ways that give residents control over their interactions. If residents have windows that look out onto a common green, for instance, they have no qualms about pulling down their interior blinds to retreat into privacy while also maintaining a literal window to the community. Front doors between individual homes are no more than 30 feet or so apart, in sharp contrast to the typical 110-foot distance between two American front doors on a conventional street.

Although Durrett was an original adherent to CNU's 1999 Charter for New Urbanism and remains in favor of the group's ongoing commentary about scale and proportion, he argues it is what happens after people move in that matters more than the size of the finials on a proper porch railing. "The village life is about knowing your neighbor better than average, which grows into caring about your neighbor more than average, and that evolves into helping your neighbor more than average," he says. "If someone falls out of bed in a cohousing community, their neighbors help them back in. If someone falls out of bed in a CNU community, they call 911." How many people living on conventional streets in conventional homes, however densely arranged, have raced to help a neighbor in this way? It does not mean they are uncaring or even unneighborly, but it does mean that the physical borders they uphold perpetuate social boundaries that may be contrary to their interests or needs.

2

Bofællesskaber and BIG at a Crossroads in Copenhagen

SHOULD 476 MARKET-RATE PRIVATE HOMES IN A HOUSING complex measuring 650,000 gross square feet be considered in a book about cohousing as we usually define the term? Not quite, for reasons of scale, economics, and the typical motives of cohousing adherents. But in considering the broader themes that define communal living and community, a discussion of scale, economics, and motives can rightfully include Bjarke Ingels Group's 8 House outside Copenhagen. It is a behemoth compared with typical cohousing communities, but

Like the rest of Ørestad, Bjarke Ingels Group's 8 House is far outside of central Copenhagen. The southern half of the neighborhood occupies a borderland between new residential housing and a nature preserve, and between the airport and the old city.

it is perfectly aligned with a design ethic that balances public and private life.

Ingels—outsized personality, founder of his eponymous firm, and a singular provocateur—might also seem like an odd fit for a book about communal living. He has been described as a restless individual who works with manic vigor. He is capable of both sophisticated treatises on "hedonistic sustain-ability" and churlish branding like the firm's website address, big.dk. He revels in incongruencies like ski-slope trash heaps or literalisms like an inflatable beer garden that takes the shape of bubbly froth. He is capable of subtle forms for iconic brands like LEGO, as well as iconic forms for discerning New Yorkers, recently delivering a vertiginous rhomboid called Via 57 West overlooking the West Side Highway. Ingels has swag-ger. He talks with his hands, and he elongates his vowels while he is doing it. He is both earnest in his intentions and shrewd in his pursuits. He is a real personality.

But his staccato ebullience conceals deeply held atti-tudes about the benefits of soberly balancing public, pri-vate, and communal lives, which is quite Danish. The Danish Ministry of Higher Education and Science entices foreign students on a website called Study in Denmark by calling it "a safe and balanced society." The Danish model and televi-sion presenter Caroline Fleming recently told the *Daily Mail* that her "Danish-ness" dictates that eating is about "balance" (and eschewing potato chips). Balance is also an overt strategy among Danes to preserve their culture while claiming open-ness to immigrants. The country is not a melting pot, in the

BIG's VM House is two structures (an *M* cosseting a *V*) made of a series of interlocking housing unit types, and The Mountain, whose south facade mirrors the angles of the underside of the *M* across the street.

parlance of other nations, but more of a bento box, with each population entitled to its own cultural milieu and customs in balance with others and adjacent to Danish culture.

In his 2004 analysis of Danish attitudes about immigration, "The Danish Cultural World of Unbridgeable Differences," the Aarhus University sociologist Peter Hervik referred to figured worlds as constellations of collective references by which we relate to each other, from archetypes like "worker" to specific characters like Hercule Poirot. These worlds are entirely personal, since we alone draw on our figured worlds to make sense of things. They are also entirely suprapersonal, since we all share the experience of working or images of Agatha Christie's gumshoe with billions of others. Figured worlds, in other words, "are embodied within a person, but are learned in social interaction over time and therefore also a product of collective history," says Hervik.

Collective history, in its virtue, might freely offer individuals characters and concepts for their figured worlds, but it also offers a panoply of definitions—all in balance, of course, with one another, but difficult to parse, especially for financial or legal ends. Contemporary debates about the production and distribution of renewable energy, for instance, have forced Danes to reinterpret the commonweal. "In Denmark, it is common to refer to community ownership, local ownership and consumer ownership, whereas the boundaries between them are blurry," say Leire Gorroño-Albizu, Karl Sperling, and Søren Djørup, in a November 2019 article for the journal *Energy Research & Social Science*. They go on to outline

Everyone gets a view and a balcony at BIG's VM House, and there are forty different residence configurations in both the V and M buildings.

The Mountain contains eighty relatively uniform apartments.

the difficulty in defining "community energy," a term caught between the Danish virtue of collectivism and the reality that the word *collective* "is not a synonym of inclusive." They point out, for instance, that "more than 60 percent of the wind companies with a collective citizen ownership in Denmark have five members or less." Separately, but as a coda to Hervik's 2004 article, collectivism has been a misleading term for immigrants to Denmark over the past two decades, who have struggled with economic and social inclusivity, to put it mildly, despite their best attempts at cultural assimilation.

Yet the balance of collectivism and individuation remains a Danish ideal—imperfect as it might be for new or even established immigrants relegated to what the Danish government calls ghettos, inchoate as it might be in inviting myriad definitions, and enduring as it might be to serve as a cultural calling card. If not an obvious advocate of this balance, Ingels has been an authentic champion. VM House (2005) and The Mountain (2007), his earliest major projects, begin to demonstrate this design ethic of accommodation, equitability for residents, and a real diversity of spaces—all values that, in one way or another, appear in the cohousing world. Both were commissioned by the entrepreneur and developer Per Høpfner, both face each other on the same street, and each is a significant project in its scale and presence in the landscape, akin to the size and scale of the Acropolis (or a little over eight acres).

The parti pris of VM House is two structures (an *M* cosseting a *V*), each made up of interlocking housing unit types, with a clever nod to Le Corbusier's Unité d'habitation in

Marseille. Everyone gets a view, there are forty different residence configurations in both buildings, and nearly everyone gets a balcony. The Mountain's form responds to VM House—its south facade mirrors the angles of the underside of the *M* across the street—and it also contains eighty relatively uniform apartments, all with views, all with outdoor terraces facing the rising sun, together constituting one-third of the program. The other two-thirds is parking for the residents, and the accommodation here is a literal one for convenience and access in what was the rather barren and desolate strip of an upstart neighborhood called Ørestad—a new development sandwiched between a suburban zone and a golf course and bisected by a major motorway.

Ingles's more recent projects also translate a sense of balance, accommodation, and equitability into other contexts. New York's 158 East 126th Street (aka The Smile), commissioned by Blumenfeld Development Group and completed in 2018, is a mix of market-rate and low-income housing, whose residents share the fitness center, coworking spaces, and modest rooftop garden that is advertised as including four pools, three of which might be better described as puddles. Copenhagen's Dortheavej (aka Frederiksborgvej 73) is an affordable, public-housing project, commissioned by the non-profit housing association Lejerbo. Although its modest budget was steered by restrictive regulations on public funding for public housing, BIG included more than twenty kinds of prefabricated residences with balconies throughout. In 2018, the Danish Association of Architects awarded its prestigious Lille

Arne Award to the Dortheavej, and news of the project's institutional recognition circulated in design media. The award signaled BIG's social bona fides within the well-intentioned but sometimes troubled legacy of social housing in Europe throughout the twentieth century, from France's habitations à loyer modéré to England's council housing flats.

South of VM House, The Mountain, and the Ørestad motorway gauntlet sits 8 House (or 8 Tallet), Denmark's largest housing project at the time of its completion in 2015, commissioned by Danish investment company St. Frederikslund Holding. Setting aside its financing and ownership model, BIG's work at 8 House signals a design ethic that makes it eligible for discussion. Like VM House, The Mountain, Dortheavej, and The Smile, 8 House is about balancing individuation and community. As the country's largest housing project, it can also rightly be its largest test site for Danish satisfaction and happiness, which routinely makes headlines, as Danes are declared the happiest people in the world—a reputation that Danish tourism and commerce agencies tout in airport banners and online marketing.

Like the rest of Ørestad, 8 House is far outside central Copenhagen, and its southern half occupies a borderland between new residential housing and a nature preserve and between the airport and the old city. Ironically, the neighborhood is as close to the country's population median center as one can get but, by all accounts, incredibly remote from the thrum of life. Not so at 8 House, which is a hive of activity. Its name derives from its figure-eight plan, but from an oblique perspective it looks more like a massive roller coaster with one corner of the eight pulled up and the opposite corner pushed down. Ingles's work has sometimes been described as "diagrammatic"—or an architectural idea that has been assigned representative forms, which is a twenty-first-century version of *architecture parlante*, or buildings that "speak" their functions, as imagined in the late eighteenth century by Claude-Nicolas Ledoux, Étienne-Louis Boullée, and Jean-Jacques Lequeu. To call it diagrammatic is entirely too simplistic for 8 House, which is defined less by its shape than by its arrangement of spaces within, all connected by a single outdoor ramp that residents say democratizes the experience of living there, as any level can be accessed without ever using the stairs or the elevator. At 8 House, BIG contained more than 650,000 square feet of residences, common areas, gardens, patios, workshops, storage, exercise rooms, and a kindergarten within one structure, and its shape owes more to Le Corbusier and Nadir Afonso's Unité d'habitation or Arturo Soria y Mata's Ciudad Lineal than it does to Ledoux's poetic if literal structures for his ideal city of Chaux. Still, BIG's 8 House does seem to be a diagram—not of an idea, but a certain quality of life that its residents are meant to achieve.

When Ila Bêka and Louise Lemoine made their film *The Infinite Happiness* about 8 House's residents in 2015, they were not coy about the project's intentions in the title, especially as it relates to the happiest country in the world. But, then again, BIG (which coproduced the film) is hardly ever coy about its projects. Bêka and Lemoine's documentary follows 8 House's

South of the Ørestad motorway gauntlet sits 8 House (8Tallet),
which could very well be Denmark's largest test site for the Danish
"happiness," which routinely makes headlines.

The 8 House is named for its figure-eight plan, but it looks
more like a massive roller coaster with one corner of the eight
pulled up and the opposite corner pushed down.

residents over twenty-one days in two dozen vignettes—its soundtrack defined by cimbasso trills and plucky strings and its mood decidedly playful. We learn about the quirks and personal philosophies of exceptionally affable people from all walks of life. Bêka and Lemoine are not necessarily fawning over the building's design so much as giving its residents a limited platform to be themselves and, in doing so, creating a generous window for us to adjudge the happiness on offer in Denmark.

"You land at Copenhagen airport, and there's a big advertisement there about happiness, and we really felt there was this incredible pressure to be happy. A collective effort to build a happy society," says Lemoine. "So, we questioned it and wondered how it works. What are the rules of happiness? What are the components to happiness?"

Bêka and Lemoine lived at 8 House while filming there, a strategy they employed for their 2014 film *Barbicania* about another megastructure, London's Barbican Centre. They have spent months shooting individual spaces and buildings by Renzo Piano, Rem Koolhaas, Herzog & de Meuron, and Gehry Partners (architecture firms that often commission them for festivals and exhibitions the firms are curating or to document specific aspects of their work), and Bêka and Lemoine are routinely hired by international luxury brands like Prada. While their portfolio is broad and the wattage of celebrity they tend to attract is rather high, the stories they tell are human ones about persistence, ambition, irony, and tenderness. One of their films is a profile of the concierge at Auguste Perret's

Film stills from *The Infinite Happiness* (2015), a film by Ila Bêka and Louise Lemoine about the residents of 8 House, south of Copenhagen.

25 bis Rue Franklin in Paris, whose daily and weekly rituals include mopping and politely dealing with architectural tourists hoping to snap photographs. Another film chronicles the work-life philosophy of the housekeeper for a private home in Bordeaux designed by Koolhaas. Another focuses on the caretaker of a remote island off the coast of Sardinia. In all, Bêka and Lemoine have made twenty-one feature-length documentary films, and in 2016, the Museum of Modern Art in New York acquired the duo's entire oeuvre for its permanent collection.

For Lemoine, the Barbican Centre and 8 House represented a turning point for their filmmaking process and a test to see if it was possible to scale up the building but keep the scale of the story intimate. "You have to be selective and so we chose a narrative system, similar to Georges Perec, suggesting the multiplicity of life about living together in the same place. The Barbican project suggested a calendar system so each day we focused on a character and a place. At 8 House, it was the building's structure that organized the film."

The structure in question is, indeed, the building itself, "pinched" as it were, into a figure eight with a cavernous inner court and capacious views for the outer apartments. The organizing structure for the building and the film is the ramp that connects the various floors, weaving in and out of the inner court and the corridors of the building itself.

For an architect of a certain vintage and training, the ramp is a datum. For an architect of another school of thought, it is a Möbius strip. Yet another architect will see it as a clever circulation solution that is wheelchair accessible. Regardless of analogy or metaphor, the result is the same for residents: everyone has a third way to get around a giant place beyond stairs and elevators, children have an all-important play space, and adults have a unique way to promenade as flaneurs or as good neighbors. That ramp is one of the keys to the building's success, remote as it is on the outskirts of Copenhagen.

The other key is something uniquely Danish. "Generally, the way the residents there understand the qualities of happiness is balance and homogeneity," says Lemoine. "Denmark being such a small country and Denmark being such a small scale European capital with wealth, it creates a sort of well calibrated population." To put it another way, there is a relative quality to happiness that might be uniquely Danish in one context but also uniquely personal in another. "Happiness is a sensation. It is not a condition. People say, 'Are you happy?' Well, I have been happy—for moments," says Fran Lebowitz in Martin Scorsese's 2010 film *Public Speaking*. (She would assuredly abhor cohousing.) Architecture might create the conditions and opportunities for the kinds of happy-making things that sustain us—like achievement, care, compassion, eating, learning, and sleeping—but those sensations are our responsibilities to experience in balance, of course, as individuals living among others.

Lemoine adds, "Being a very recent building, it's a very recent community, and the success of it depends on social homogeneity and shared expectation in terms of a lifestyle. That's why the building works pretty well. Tensions appear,

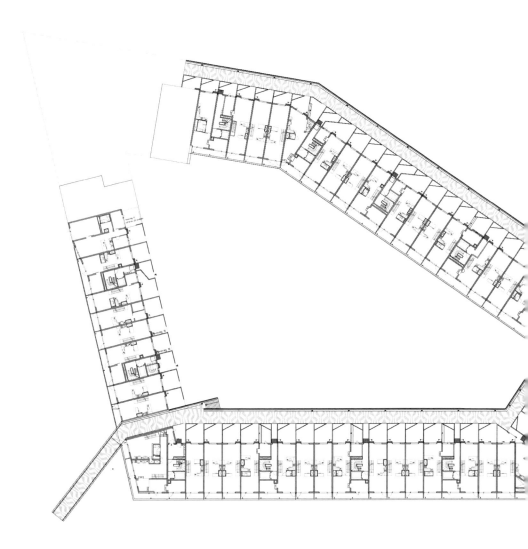

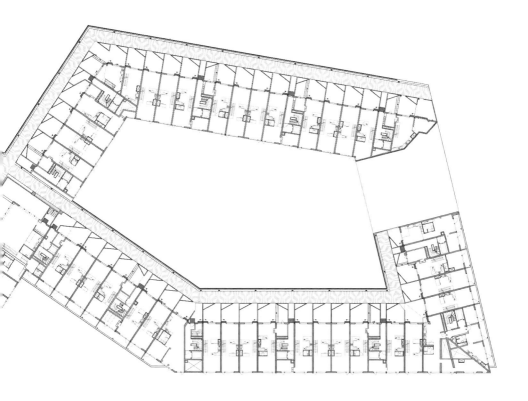

The ramp of 8 House is the organizing structure of a design pinched into a figure eight and weaves in and out, as seen in the plan for the first level of rowhouses. The ramp narrows and widens based on the level and represents a datum, a Mobius strip, or a thread depending on one's disposition.

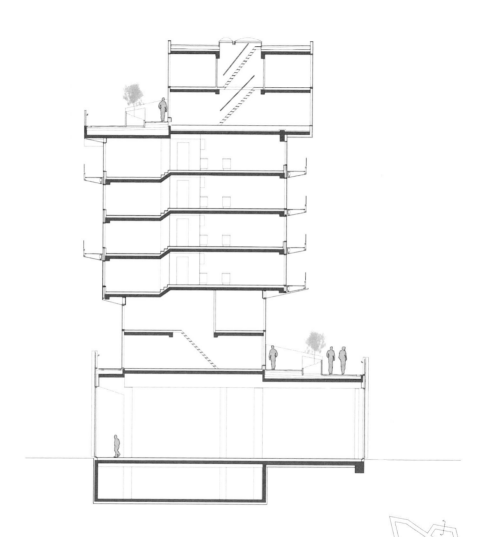

Above and opposite: Section drawings of 8 House

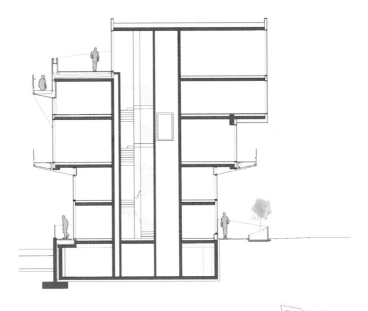

yes, and you can have microcommunities within communities, and you can have intense relationships in solidarity, but [these] are all real aspects [of community]. There is a feeling of harmony there [because] they are all looking for certain values based on communal experience."

BOFAELLESSKABER

The Danish word *hygge* has had its moment in the sun (or its moment by a roaring fire) in the last few years, and the coziness and "comfortable conviviality" of *hygge* have become important cultural exports for a country that is slightly bigger than Maryland and slightly smaller than West Virginia. *Bofaellesskaber* is a lesser-known export, but an important moment for cohousing as coined by Charles Durrett and Kathryn McCamant in their landmark 1988 study *Cohousing: A Contemporary Approach to Housing Ourselves*, based on their survey of nearly fifty Danish communities formed in the 1970s and early 1980s. Translated as "living together," *bofaellesskaber* defines the circumstance of living with others, as many of us do, but it also defines the circumstance of living among others, as we all do. By 1993 (and the book's second edition), Durrett and McCamant estimated that more than 140 self-defined, self-administered communities had succeeded in Denmark. Ranging from six to forty household families, they included rural communities, like Trudeslund in Birkerød or Gyndbjerg in Bjert, and urban communities, like nine conjoined row houses in Aarhus called Jerngarden. They identified common characteristics that made *bofaellesskaber* work, such as a participatory process, intentional neighborhood design (or planned communities), extensive common facilities, and complete resident management. In doing so, they literally wrote the book on cohousing by giving it a name and recognizable qualities that are part of the vocabulary of participatory design and its outcomes. What they did not do, however, was narrowly define cohousing as an insouciant idyll overtaken by hemp plants where nothing is owned and everyone is free to live beyond the berm of acceptable social norms. Cohousing residents, to the contrary, are highly organized and principled people who openly acknowledge the need to balance individual needs and interests with collective values and goals. This structured approach to living is inherently spatial, if not architectural, and some scholars refer to it as social architecture (but not necessarily socialist architecture). For Durrett and McCamant, "cohousing refers to an idea about how people can live together, rather than any particular financing or ownership type. Other than determining who can afford to live in the development, financing makes little difference in the actual function of cohousing. Thus cohousing differs from other housing categories, such as cooperatives and condominiums, which are defined by their type of ownership."

Communal living, as a broad, encompassing umbrella term, then, is based on the idea that the things that sustain us as individuals, such as food, shelter, and familial ties, are better when they are shared, which erodes the border between our private and public lives, between personal interests and group dynamics, that we tend to uphold. While it does not go as far as cohousing to suggest an ownership model, covenants, or community rules, the term *communal living* is robust enough to signal a way of living distinct from conventional norms of homeownership that use visible and invisible borders to enforce social barriers. Residents may encircle their property with walls and fences (or even a moat) to keep people out. They may plant enormous evergreens to thwart nosy neighbors. Maybe they have adopted guard dogs. Maybe they have even constructed a legal barrier to limit their liability by purchasing property and paying utilities as a limited liability company. Conventional homeowners find ways to insulate themselves from others (and from others knowing their business), which we colloquially regard as the quintessence of privacy.

As a counterpoint to privacy, we create spaces of conviviality on a spectrum of fully public to semiprivate, including libraries, parks, plazas, shopping centers, and café terraces, which are all seen as hallmarks of civility. Pandemic be damned, we may choose to attend block parties or neighborhood barbecues, happy hours, and tenant gatherings. In large cities, sidewalks and streets remain public with equal rights of access for everyone, from everyday commuters or occasional protestors, as they skirt semiprivate or fully private properties. Some property owners see social and financial advantages to making concessions to the public, as with the privately owned public spaces (POPS) in New York and London. Others see advantages in gifting their land for public use in perpetuity, as with Mitchell Park in Washington, DC, or Grange Park in Toronto.

Yet these well-trodden paths of civility where notions of what is public and what is private seem perfectly clear (even if the liminal zones of POPS) also exist within the broad term *community living* and the more specific term *cohousing*. From Trudeslund to Jerngarden, or even from Fair Oaks in Sacramento to Takoma Village Cohousing outside Washington, DC, *bofaellesskaber* is defined in practice as living together, but not at the expense of one's privacy or one's need for sociability. What is different are the motives of the individuals within their communities, whether they are environmental, faith-based, economic, or social. But at base level and in its Danish origin, *bofaellesskaber* seeks efficiencies to eliminate the "impracticalities of single-family houses and apartment units," as Durrett and McCamant have written, and instead "combine the autonomy of private dwellings with the advantages of community living."

Still, ownership matters, even if individual motives are held in balance with the community's interests. But what are communal living or even cohousing advocates actually owning in exchange for their investments of time and money, as well as their vested interest in one another? Durrett and McCamant identified the first cohousing community at Saettedammen, which was established by twenty-seven families outside Copenhagen in 1972, and another, a year later, at Skråplanet, whose residents were seeking to upend conventional definitions of family, according to Henrik Gutzon Larsen, a geographer at Lund University. The upheaval of the late 1960s, *kollektivhuset* (collective housing) in Sweden, and the golden age of Soviet-style communism created a geographic and social milieu in which everything from home economics to child development was up for debate in Denmark. Ownership (or, as Larsen calls it, tenure) was an important part of the cultural debate about economic mobility in Denmark as a function of fairness and access, and whether a roof over one's head should be regarded as a commodity for trading or as a fundamental human right. "In Denmark," says Larsen, "a community based on cooperative tenure can prioritize the access of younger people to an aging community. This is not possible in owner-occupied communities, where units are exchanged individually on the private-property market."

Larsen's collective tenure, as a status that transcends present-day legal rights and financial security to be a larger, multigenerational concept, comes to bear on the deeper quest to achieve and maintain a particular quality of life based on balancing individuation and collectivism—to be enjoyed now and in the future. It is apparent in the stories of Bêka and Lemoine's *Infinite Happiness*, from the blind piano tuner to the volunteer handyman squad, whose personal philosophies meld with notions of public welfare. It is central to Ingels's concepts of "hedonistic sustainability" and "social infrastructure" to maximize personal enjoyment in the context of communal gain regardless of site constraints or environmental threats. Ownership is really a debate about the exigencies of living together, which also transcends law and money, as we structure our lives to live with people we want to (or need to) at any cost. Or, as the Newcastle University geographer Helen

Jarvis noted in a recent study of cohousing on three continents, living together is an arrangement of "social architecture" that is more enduring than market conditions. As social architecture, living together is a design ethic that demands a balance between the barriers of private life and the commons of social life—two spheres that must accommodate each other, as we must all accommodate one another, for a greater good.

3

3

The Ecological Imperative

STATISTICS COMPILED BY THE FOUNDATION FOR INTENTIONAL Community (FIC), founded in 1937, shed light on the characteristics of intentional communities worldwide: it lists 467 cohousing communities, defined as those organized by individual homes within a group-owned property, and 465 ecovillages globally, defined as those organized around ecology and sustainability. The overlap between the two groups is significant. By the foundation's count, 588 intentional communities worldwide operate as group-owned properties occupied by individuals who prioritize sustainability and ecology. By comparison, the foundation recognizes 229 Christian cohousing communities and 128 Jewish cohousing communities, which seem to be rather low tallies considering their pervasiveness as global religions. These figures are also not inclusive of combinations such as Judaic ecovillages that operate on a cohousing model and not a commune model, for instance. Suffice it to say that the ecological imperative is a secular driver of cohousing motives, and sustainability defines a legacy of the cohousing movement writ large.

Over the years, FIC has tracked intentional communities and served as a hub for classified ads, event listings, and information. Its list is not exhaustive, but it is one of the only attempts to account for the growing popularity of intentional communities—if perhaps a rather US-centric one, even if intentional communities are as American as cohousing communities are Danish. In a *New York Times* story from January 2020, Mike Mariani translated the American experience in democracy as a specifically American laboratory to develop alternative living, from the Puritans and Pilgrims in the seventeenth century to the Transcendentalists in the 1830s, the offshoot Unitarian communities around New England, the artist colonies and collectives from nineteenth-century New Hampshire, and twentieth-century California retreats. Mariani explored the theme of conversion throughout his piece—how the call of some purpose-driven life in an intentional community still requires even the most fervent individual to relinquish habits and notions of ownership. Quoting

Around the myth of Arcosanti in Arizona, hundreds of communities have cropped up in the last forty years that address the ecological imperative to live responsibly within nature.

Henry David Thoreau's line from *Walden*, "He will live with the license of a higher order of things," Mariani concluded that "there will always, however, be the daunting task of letting go."

Within architecture, the Arcosanti community in Cordes Junction, Arizona, is arguably the best-known intentional community, which routinely draws thousands of visitors a year to examine the silt-cast structures, participate in ceramic bell-making classes, and marvel at the community itself, driven for years and in equal parts through the sheer will of its founder, Paolo Soleri, and the commitment of its residents to living in an environmentally friendly way. Around the myth of Arcosanti, its governing Cosanti Foundation, or even Soleri's "Arcology" philosophy that architecture and ecology are one and the same, hundreds of communities have cropped up in the last forty years that address the ecological imperative to live responsibly within nature. Admittedly, these communities do not reach the levels of theoretical sophistication of Arcology or the otherworldly architectural coherence of Arcosanti. They do define, however, a spectrum of possibility for everyday people looking to make a change in the way they live while making their lifestyle an exemplar.

FAIR OAKS ECOHOUSING, SACRAMENTO, CALIFORNIA

Fair Oaks EcoHousing, designed by McCamant & Durrett Architects (known today as the Cohousing Company), broke ground in 2017, a year in which the United States announced

Fair Oaks EcoHousing, designed by McCamant & Durrett Architects, broke ground in Fair Oaks, California, in 2017, and embodies the idea that living by example is the best way of leading by example.

The site plan of Fair Oaks EcoHousing is defined by a central pedestrian-only lane with individual houses in proximity. At the midpoint is a common house, and its frontage to the street is limited to a modest driveway.

its planned exit from the Paris Agreement, Congress passed a bill allowing for fossil-fuel extraction in Alaska's Arctic National Wildlife Refuge, and the Environmental Protection Agency began dismantling the Obama-era Clean Power Plan. The Trump administration took a dozen other anti-environmental actions that year (and in subsequent years), and together they represented categorical assaults against the global community, against the strong ethos of environmental conservation in the United States, and against future genera-tions. Something called eco-housing, then, would at the very least seem to be a rejoinder to the hostility of climate deniers, but Fair Oaks is not quite that blatant. In fact, it is understated in its quiet environmentalism, embodying the idea that living by example is the best way of leading by example.

What is the example, then, at Fair Oaks? How to margin-alize the car to make it an accessory. The average car emits about nineteen pounds of carbon dioxide and other gasses from the tailpipe for every gallon of gasoline burned, which does not count the five pounds that comes from extraction, production, and delivery of the fuel, according to the Union of Concerned Scientists. With thirty units at Fair Oaks and as many (if not more) cars, CO_2 savings start to add up.

Marty Maskall, who cofounded Fair Oaks, reports that residents use their cars far less than they would if they lived more conventional lives in suburbia and exurbia, as she once did. "I used to drive my car two or three times a day, and now I go two or three days without even looking at my car," says Maskall. "Our residents just choose to be here. People don't

The flats and townhomes at Fair Oaks EcoHousing have five different floor plans, each with two to four bedrooms, that feature open concept plans illuminated by large windows that maximize natural light.

have to go out to dinner because we cook for each other. There is more sharing and it's easier to coordinate rides."

The site plan of Fair Oaks EcoHousing is defined by a central pedestrian-only lane, off of which individual houses sit in proximity. At the midpoint is a common house for meals, events, group functions, and meetings, with an eating area, kitchen, playroom, laundry room, music room, and guest quarters. Its frontage to New York Avenue in the northeast suburbs of Sacramento is limited to a modest driveway, from which a line of garages extends due west, allowing residents to park their vehicles before continuing on to their homes beyond, situated on a north-south axis. This car-free procession in part distinguishes Fair Oaks, along with other communities pursuing a streetscape defined by the human scale. Some were designed to eschew cars, with a New Urbanist argument about a "real neighborhood" in mind, while others, just as explicitly, marginalize cars as a carbon-reduction and air-quality-improvement strategy. Other aspects of Fair Oaks make it an intentionally sustainable community in its own right, beyond architectural ideologies, for an environmentally vulnerable part of the United States. The community includes five types of private homes, from two- to four-bedroom layouts, which feature open-concept spaces illuminated by large windows that maximize natural light. In section, it is what the project's architects call a green wall, with FSC-certified wood trusses and floors, fly ash and concrete slabs, recycled flooring materials, and low-emissivity windows that keep the interiors warmer in the winter by refracting some rays, and cooler in the summer by reflecting other rays.

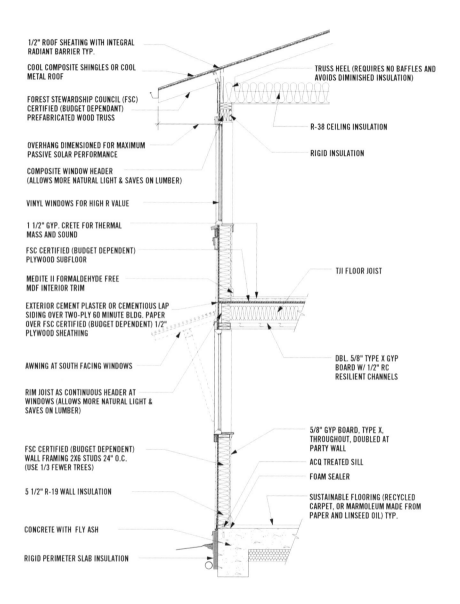

1/2" ROOF SHEATING WITH INTEGRAL RADIANT BARRIER TYP.

COOL COMPOSITE SHINGLES OR COOL METAL ROOF

FOREST STEWARDSHIP COUNCIL (FSC) CERTIFIED (BUDGET DEPENDANT) PREFABRICATED WOOD TRUSS

OVERHANG DIMENSIONED FOR MAXIMUM PASSIVE SOLAR PERFORMANCE

COMPOSITE WINDOW HEADER (ALLOWS MORE NATURAL LIGHT & SAVES ON LUMBER)

VINYL WINDOWS FOR HIGH R VALUE

1 1/2" GYP. CRETE FOR THERMAL MASS AND SOUND

FSC CERTIFIED (BUDGET DEPENDENT) PLYWOOD SUBFLOOR

MEDITE II FORMALDEHYDE FREE MDF INTERIOR TRIM

EXTERIOR CEMENT PLASTER OR CEMENTIOUS LAP SIDING OVER TWO-PLY 60 MINUTE BLDG. PAPER OVER FSC CERTIFIED (BUDGET DEPENDENT) 1/2" PLYWOOD SHEATHING

AWNING AT SOUTH FACING WINDOWS

RIM JOIST AS CONTINUOUS HEADER AT WINDOWS (ALLOWS MORE NATURAL LIGHT & SAVES ON LUMBER)

FSC CERTIFIED (BUDGET DEPENDENT) WALL FRAMING 2X6 STUDS 24" O.C. (USE 1/3 FEWER TREES)

5 1/2" R-19 WALL INSULATION

CONCRETE WITH FLY ASH

RIGID PERIMETER SLAB INSULATION

TRUSS HEEL (REQUIRES NO BAFFLES AND AVOIDS DIMINISHED INSULATION)

R-38 CEILING INSULATION

RIGID INSULATION

TJI FLOOR JOIST

DBL. 5/8" TYPE X GYP BOARD W/ 1/2" RC RESILIENT CHANNELS

5/8" GYP BOARD, TYPE X, THROUGHOUT, DOUBLED AT PARTY WALL

ACQ TREATED SILL

FOAM SEALER

SUSTAINABLE FLOORING (RECYCLED CARPET, OR MARMOLEUM MADE FROM PAPER AND LINSEED OIL) TYP.

The homes at Fair Oaks are constructed with FSC-certified wood trusses and floors, fly ash and concrete slabs, recycled flooring materials, and low-emissivity windows.

Fair Oaks's sustainability principles are rooted in the broader spirit of responsible living, but they are also rooted in the environmental challenges of California's Central Valley. Rolling blackouts in August 2020 were reminiscent of the energy crisis of 2000–2001, when drought diminished hydro-electric power, stressing already low reserves, and sent prices soaring. As a result, the debate about energy dependence is also about how sustainability should push beyond conservation to address environmental vulnerabilities caused by climate change, in turn caused by carbon reliance.

The myth of the "rugged" American West belies the fact that it is a patchwork of delicate landscapes and ecotones far more susceptible to climate changes than mythmaking about ruggedness would have us believe. Sacramento is such a place. It is a river city between the Pacific Ocean to the west and a chain of national forests abutting the Nevada border to the east that cosset its valley in a ring of green. Increasingly over the last forty years, it has been a ring of fire, however. Higher temperatures during the dry season mean more water evaporates from the ground, exacerbating the dryness and creating the tinderbox effect that Californians dread each year. Over the last generation, the amount of acreage burned annually has increased fivefold due to anthropogenic climate change, according to a 2019 study in the journal *Earth's Future*. Summer blazes that rip through timberland and continue to smolder in pockets through the early fall have increased in size by nearly 800 percent, increasing the amount of acreage incinerated and decreasing the effectiveness of wildland firefighters. In August

2020, Lake Berryessa, roughly forty-five minutes by car to the west of Sacramento, was completely encircled by a wildfire thirty-five miles long by twenty-five miles wide. That was only one of eight simultaneously active incidents in a state that had seen more than 1.4 million acres destroyed in the previous three months.

A less car-reliant neighborhood, then, seems like a reasonable step to reducing carbon, especially around Sacramento. "Our association of Fair Oaks in Sacramento in this part of California means, to me, that we're doing something useful," says Maskall, who notes that a communal agreement about environmental awareness through carbon reduction and walkability—not just an individual consumer's casual attitudes—keeps people honest about their habits. In 2016, the Environmental Council of Sacramento recognized Maskall for founding Fair Oaks with a pedestrian-first focus as the basis of resident interaction—shunting cars to the periphery and privileging face-to-face conversation at the scale of the human body.

"Basically, I saw cohousing and decided it was a better way to live," she says. "I see that some people understand the concept immediately, but others not as quickly. In the suburbs, we were isolated, we whizzed by each other, we didn't have porches. Now, though, I have neighbors I know, I have a porch. Although COVID-19 has prevented us from using our common areas as fully as we'd like, we still get together on the terrace."

There are some compelling precedents for this idea going back to early reports of automobile fatalities in the first decades of the twentieth century. Perhaps the most compelling concept is Louis Kahn's 1952 proposal for Philadelphia, where private automobiles were to be checked at the periphery in parking structures encircling the downtown core between the Delaware and Schuylkill Rivers. He allowed trucks and busses limited access, but the message of privileging foot traffic over all else was clear. Since then, members of the Congress for the New Urbanism (CNU) have advanced this idea (and others that constitute its charter) as an order of magnitude: regional economic power citywide and neighborhood cohesion, which promote civility at the most human scale at the block and street level. Kahn's 1971 speech "The Room, the Street, and Human Agreement" even identifies the room, "a place of the mind," as the scale that we all innately understand and the basis of our experience at larger scales. This idea that the scale of the body in space is the basis of civility—and, by extension, effective urbanism—is the basis of the work of a founder of CNU, Peter Calthorpe, whose firm Calthorpe Associates, acquired in 2019 by Omaha-based HDR, has designed and built hundreds of buildings with this in mind since its founding in 1983.

A twenty-minute drive from Fair Oaks to downtown Sacramento, however, stands Sim Van der Ryn's 1978 commission with Calthorpe for a four-story office building that might not have been an architectural model for Maskall's pedestrian-centric community but serves as a conceptual model for

The atrium of Sim Van der Ryn and Peter Calthorpe's Bateson Building in Sacramento, California, pulls hot air down on cool days and pushes hot air up (and out) on warm days; it's known as the building's "lung." Its visible and more obvious value is as an amenity for gathering— "an indoor plaza," says the architect Michael Bednar.

passive cooling's capabilities at scale. The Bateson Building's core is an atrium without air-conditioning, which was audacious for a city that routinely goes above one hundred degrees in August and September. The atrium pulls hot air down on cool days and pushes hot air up (and out) on warm days, earning it an occasional moniker as the building's "lung." Louvers on the outside regulate solar heat gain, and more than six hundred tons of rock beneath the atrium absorb and store thermal energy, which can be released via vaporizers and fans to acclimate the building. Using these tactics, the architects imagined that the Bateson Building could reduce its energy costs by at least three-quarters over its lifetime and recoup the cost of construction within a generation. But those oft-publicized benefits remain hidden. Its visible and more obvious value is as an amenity for gathering—"an indoor plaza" and "a conducive social setting," the architect Michael Bednar wrote a decade later—for state government workers on their lunch break and passersby going to or from adjacent Roosevelt Park. To borrow Kahn's phrase, the atrium's form and function is both a room and a street, simultaneously and literally at the Bateson Building, as well as at Fair Oaks. As the basis of social sustainability, the scale of the street plays a vital role in the success of cohousing projects, along with proportion and purpose. But what about the size of the community? How does proportion and purpose play out when the scale of the community itself is reduced?

COASTAL COHOUSING, MAINE

Six individuals are a small group by cohousing standards and may yet be the smallest unit of analysis if the optimal size of a cohousing community is twenty to forty-five people, according to cohousing advocates. However, both the design process and the finished outcome provide more than enough evidence that consensus and collaboration are enduring features of cohousing's unwritten philosophy. In the case of this ten-thousand-square-foot project in Maine's most populous region, consensus and collaboration also defined the friend group of three couples who spent the better part of a decade vacationing together and refining their group dynamic, which led to a desire to live together in retirement and semiretirement.

It is hard to imagine six people so obviously committed to each other, so intentional in nurturing that commitment, and so methodical in pursuing an architectural analogue to their friendship based on collective trust and mutual respect. But that is precisely what this group is about—not to mention a healthy dose of discretion in terms of not allowing too many identifying details to be published. "People think it's a novelty. They think we're a novelty," says one member of the community. "All six of us knew we were committed to each other's growth, development, and stake in our community of six. It's why we wanted to live together. To continue that growth."

This project sits between Portland and Brunswick on the southern coast of Maine, nestled behind big barrier islands that guard against the Atlantic's swells and smaller islands that quell the breakers off Casco Bay and create conditions for both

Designed by Richard Renner, this coastal cohousing project consists of three connected homes with shared amenities intended for six individuals. It's small by cohousing standards but remains an effective unit for analysis.

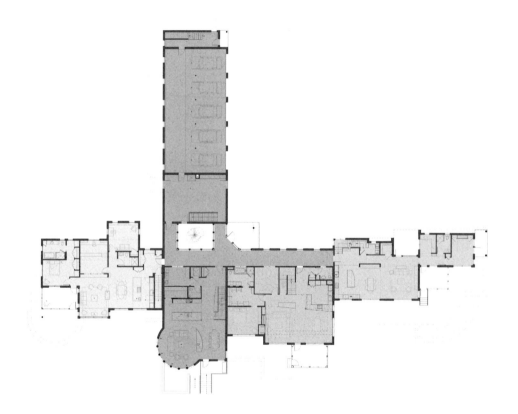

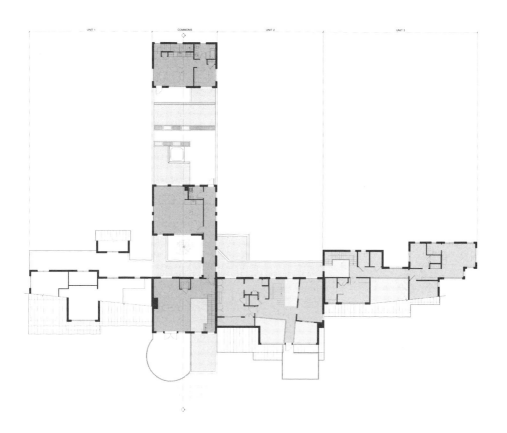

In plan, Renner's coastal cohousing forms a T—its wings containing three distinct living quarters and its stem containing the shared amenities, such as an art studio, garage, library, workout room, and media room.

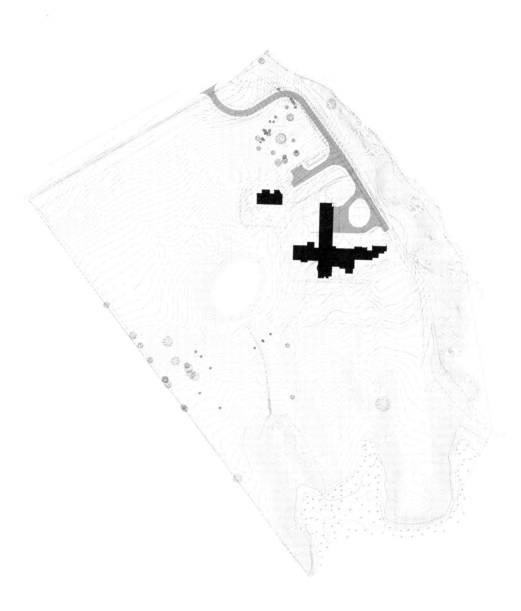

The three units of coastal cohousing have unique and uninterrupted
southern exposures overlooking more than sixteen acres
of mudflats in one direction and upland scrubby pines in another.

an ideal harbor and an ideal mill community fed by a forty-mile-long river. Designed by the architect Richard Renner, the project consists of three homes connected by a common house that opens onto a shared garage and an additional apartment initially designed for a caretaker and sometimes used as guest quarters. In plan, the entire structure forms a *T*, whose wings contain the three distinct living quarters and whose stem contains the shared amenities, such as an art studio, library, workout room, and media room. The living quarters range from eighteen hundred square feet to three thousand square feet, corresponding to the means and budget of each couple, and have distinct configurations devised, in some cases, with the help of interior architects recommended by Renner. This last concession involving multiple designers was more about time than anything else, as the project took only sixteen months from start to finish.

"One of the key issues for this group was that balance between having a place to be by themselves, but also having the architecture create a range of possibilities to gather, subtle or otherwise," says Renner. The stem of the *T* contains the single entry hallway for all three homes from a shared garage. Beyond this entry procession, however, community members have as much privacy as they wish to have, a design value that even extends to the viewshed. Nestled along the property's flank, the three units have unique and uninterrupted southern exposures overlooking more than sixteen acres of mudflats in one direction and upland scrubby pines in the other. Most of the property is a conservation easement, which works

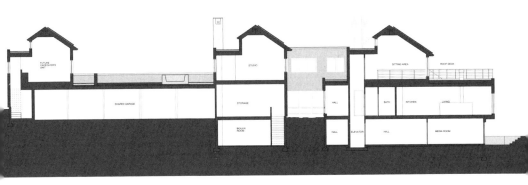

The coastal Maine cohousing project hugs the edge of its property in observance of the natural landscape beyond, and it participates in the broader vernacular of farm buildings and barns. For Renner and his clients, it was important that the project felt residential. Even if the accoutrements of a single-family house, like chimneys, weren't necessary, Renner designed them to function as ventilation while making the roof line appear domestic in nature.

in tandem with a zoning rule allowing for a zero lot line for condominium construction if a majority of the land is left as open space. "Animals [that] we didn't know lived here before we bought the land pass through here all the time. Wild turkeys, wolves, herons, and egrets. I mean, it was a field that's their home, and now it's conservation land, too," says one of the community members, who wishes to remain anonymous. "Our footprint is here now, and there are river birches that have grown around us, and so we sit in the land in ways we couldn't have imagined at first."

"We started by working inside out, which is to say with design values at first, with the public-private realm and the intersection of the two," says Renner. The process of marrying community values and architectural form was also a negotiation. "We also had to work from the outside in, because we were not interested in building a diagram. Of course, there would be an underlying diagram of how the residents wanted to live, but it would be a guiding factor only."

Renner's particular approach to balancing inside-out and outside-in approaches to shaping space is, by his admission, influenced by his studies at the Massachusetts Institute of Technology in the early 1970s, as well as the work of the architects Aldo van Eyck, Alvar Aalto, and Herman Hertzberger, who started his eponymous firm in 1958 (now known as AAH). These reference points can be combined in several ways to form rich legacies in architecture, urbanism, architectural education, and graphic design, but the unifying thread for Renner and others is simply using human behavior and group dynamics as the genesis of understanding space. Plan, section, and elevation drawings reflect the human units of analysis instead of driving faceless programming or suggesting hierarchies of function. "There's a real sense of designing for the collective good in this project," says Renner, "and I think that's something always worth designing for."

Each of the original three couples came to the table as equal partners in the design process, even if they were unevenly positioned financially. "Early on, we understood that we were not equally resourced as couples. We all brought something to the project that was equally valuable, not just money. Some had money, some had time; some had imagination, some had pragmatism," says one of the residents, noting that while they were tightly knit as a group of longtime friends, the process of designing a home required the input of Renner and other design consultants who understood the balance between communal values, personal equity, and spatial design. "The one thing I want to be said about us is, 'Six was not enough,'" she says.

In addition to Renner and interior architects, the community worked with the landscape architecture firm Terrence J. DeWan & Associates, as well as a project coordinator who acted as a kind of ombudsperson and facilitator during critical phases of the project. In the end, the project does not look like a compound or a community or even anything out of the ordinary from the outside, which is precisely what Renner imagined would be an important feature to align with both the local vernacular and the landscape. "It was important that it looked residential. The chimneys aren't chimneys. They're ventilation, but they're placed in such a way that makes sense [with] where you'd expect to see a chimney form on the outside," he says. "The biggest thing about vernacular is size and scale. When I think of vernacular, I think of intimacy. One of the things we talked about was to assemble a collection of farm buildings."

Renner's regard for the modestly sized everyday structures of the area limits the physical footprint of the project on the land and helps reconcile the immediate context with ten thousand square feet of new construction. At first glance, it is not immediately apparent that the design of this cohousing project is an act of conservation. The site plan tells the real story of this structure, essentially pushed to one corner of a wild and vibrant landscape. It is an arrangement that Hertzberger, one of Renner's influences, would recognize. "When you leave your house, you should come into another space but a space of another nature," said Hertzberger in a 2017 interview, "one that implies you always see a horizon, you see the next thing."

SUDERBYN, GOTLAND, SWEDEN

Some cohousing groups see conservation in active terms rather than under the banner of permaculture centered on regenerative agriculture, "rewilding," and establishing community behaviors around these processes. Permaculture is about intervention, but only to the extent that intervention facilitates the resilience of natural ecosystems. Suderbyn Permaculture Ecovillage was founded in 2008 on cooperatively purchased land. From its start in an extant farmhouse and barn, it has grown to a small village of several new and rehabilitated structures, including a greenhouse for the winter garden and an adjacent (and expansive) plot for the summer garden. As an ecovillage, its allure is not necessarily about how architecture facilitates group living in the way that Arcosanti does in its assemblage of silt-cast and concrete structures or about a singular design vision like Paolo Soleri's Arcology. Suderbyn's allure is how a way of living spurs the adaptation of vernacular and agricultural structures. Its geodesic dome is the only hint of the elysian future imagined by Buckminster Fuller seventy years ago. However, there is one thing that unites Arcosanti and Suderbyn: residents must abandon notions of conventional living to make them work in a long-term way.

All the food available at Suderbyn is vegan, prepared each day by one or two people in a rotation. Neither drugs nor hard liquor is allowed. The community is wary of what its members call medical residues left by pharmaceuticals, hormones, or antibiotics, so a dedicated toilet is available for visitors or members who must ingest them. Everyone else uses the compost toilet, capped with a wooden lid. Visitors may rent a tent or a bed in a room (as well as pay a food fee) for any length of time, but they receive a significant discount for month-long stays, which Suderbyn calls test living. Volunteering also reduces a visitor's costs. Permanent residents must volunteer at least ten hours per week, although they typically do more, and work at least four hours per day on construction, cleaning, gardening, organizing, or administering the community.

From its start in a farmhouse and barn, Suderbyn Permaculture Ecovillage, on the Swedish Island of Gotland, has grown to a small village of several new and rehabilitated structures and spaces, including a greenhouse for the winter garden and an expansive plot for the summer garden.

The Suderbyn community is wary of what its members refer to as medical residues from pharmaceuticals, hormones, or antibiotics, so a dedicated toilet is available for visitors or members who must ingest them. Everyone else uses the compost toilet, capped with a wooden lid with a handle.

Permanent membership requires a one-time donation of 10,000 SEK (or about $1,100) and a refundable contribution of 5,000 SEK (about $564), as well as a signed pledge to abide by Suderbyn's principles.

While many co-living communities in the United States exist legally as condominium units, the glue that holds them together is their codes of conduct and communal values. Suderbyn's co-living principles are more prescriptive, ranging from what people eat and how they may address each other in conversation to the ways in which they may earn a living. Its principles state, in part, "Suderbyn does not have one specific spiritual path," yet it reveres the social contracts found at the monastic end of the spectrum. At the heart of the community is what its residents call "deep participatory governance" as defined by Sociocracy 3.0 (S3), a system of thinking and acting derived from the nineteenth-century philosophy of Auguste Comte, later adapted by the Dutch pacifist Kees Boeke in the late 1920s and early 1930s as a pedagogical model for children at his Children's Community Workshop in Bilthoven and as a management model for organizations (owing something to Quaker methods of communal decision-making). Eventually, it was interpreted as a seven-part code of conduct by the Dutch electrical engineer Gerard Endenburg as the Sociocratic Circle Organisation Method. Anyone who has written and signed planned performance goals required by their employer at any time in the last two decades will recognize S3, which asks for transparency, continuous improvement, effectiveness, and accountability. Not as frequently co-opted by corporate

While many co-living communities in the US exist legally as condominium units, the glue that holds them together is their codes of conduct and communal values. Sweden's Suderbyn co-living community is guided by principles that are far more prescriptive, ranging from what people eat and how they may address each other in conversation to the ways in which they may earn a living.

culture, but vital to S3 nonetheless, are "equivalence" (ensuring equal voices for all in decision-making), "empiricism" (letting a rational process guide debate), and "consent" (seeking unanimity by addressing objections to improve the outcome).

Using this rubric, Suderbyn is legally structured as a living cooperative (Suderbyn People-Care), a foundation (Suderbyn Earth-Care), and an NGO called RELEARN Suderbyn. It is also socially structured around a few foundational areas such as "consumption," which is to say that Suderbyn takes a staunch anti–mass consumption position by purchasing organic, seasonal, and fair trade food (when its residents are not growing their own), securing only biodegradable products, and aggressively reusing or recycling everything. The second is "violence and personal development," which is a call for civility and acceptance. The third is "religion and ideology," which accepts all faiths and political positions, and even encourages political action, so long as they are not oriented toward violence. There is also "entrepreneurship," which limits residents to "green businesses which contribute to broader positive change in society and in Suderbyn, itself."

Suderbyn is perhaps on the extreme end of the spectrum of ecological living and prescriptive communal and individual behaviors, and it is not for everyone, even if everyone might benefit from spending a few days there. There are another 456 established or emerging ecovillages across fifty countries that forge a middle ground in cultivating community in a demonstratively sustainable way. Some of them have been conceived and designed at the intersection of environmental and economic sustainability to define what affordable could mean outside the trappings of middle-class life. Others set up educational demonstrations at which a few committed residents work with school groups, at-risk youth groups, and church groups on both the principles of conservation and their capacity for social or even spiritual rehabilitation.

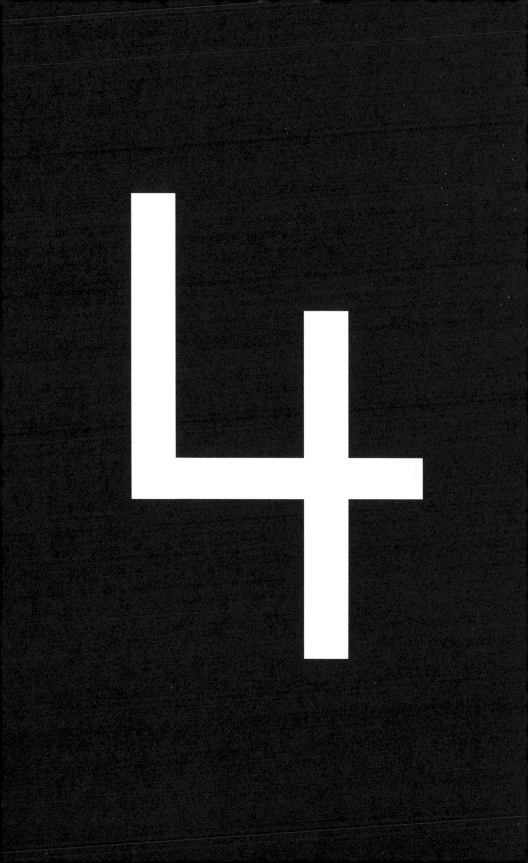

4

Independent Living
and Third-Age Housing

THE CATCH-ALL TERM *SENIOR LIVING* ENCOMPASSES A RANGE of options in the United States, from independent living for active Americans "fifty-five or better," as the phrase goes, to assisted living scenarios for those with infirmities who need daily or even hourly attention. The term does a poor job of conveying how many different types of group living arrangements are available to seniors. It also does a poor job of defining *senior*. Some people may self-identify as a senior when they turn sixty (although some senior discounts can be claimed beginning at age fifty-five), while others may do so when their first partial Social Security benefits check arrives at sixty-two, yet the ultimate arbiter may well be age seventy-two, when mandatory benefits withdrawals begin.

Semantics aside, senior-living communities have never been as large of a market sector or more lucrative for the companies that own them in any point in their history than today. One recent report by the Business Research Company claims the global retirement community market reached a value of more than $218 billion in 2019, growing 8.6 percent since 2015, and expected to achieve an annual growth rate of 9.8 percent to more than $317 billion by 2023. The Senior Housing division of the American commercial real estate group CBRE noted in a 2019 report that better health care has improved mortality rates and survivorship rates. In the same report, the group projected that, by 2030, about 21 percent (or 56.1 million) of the US population will be age sixty-five or older, and by 2050, 85.6 million people will be within that bracket—a 50 percent increase over today.

Proportionate increases can be found across the same span of time for the sixty-plus set in many other countries too. Since the mid-1980s, upward of 250 senior living or third-age communities have been established by their residents in Denmark, yet they remain largely unpublicized and unknown. The anthropologist Max Pedersen lamented in one 2015 study that although Danish cohousing projects have represented a pilgrimage route for architects worldwide, the senior-living communities among them have been largely ignored. Only two Danish studies have been published on the subject since 2000, both by Pedersen's Danish Building Research Institute, and there is a dearth of information about who is motivated to join a third-age cohousing community there, what those motives might be, and how the idea (and the ideal) of community translates to quality of life for people of the oldest generation, who are often marginalized.

Gerontologists generally lament the lack of regard for older citizens among so-called prime-age citizens and youth between the ages of twenty-five and fifty-four, particularly in the West. The expression "having a senior moment," as mild as it seems, is just the beginning of recognizing ageism, which the American Psychological Association states takes deeper and more structural forms including "prejudicial attitudes, discriminatory practices, or institutional policies and practices that perpetuate stereotypical beliefs," in its 2020 Resolution on Ageism. Surveys conducted by psychologists over the years routinely return grim results in that the majority of older citizens experience ageism. The common assumption is that because one is old, one must be impaired in some way, and therefore avoided or treated differently. Older citizens live in what psychologists have termed "the invisible years."

As a partial result, depression, loneliness, and struggles with sociability are well-known challenges of growing older (although not solely a function of old age). As a counterpoint, being an active part of a community can stem some of those challenges, as has been widely documented. Seniors considered highly social are more likely to overcome depressive symptoms, their cognitive decline slows markedly, and their motor functions remain stronger for longer through old age. The Royal Institute of British Architects called older Britons "consumers of culture and experience" in its 2019 report "Silver Linings," which features six urban futures for Britons with proportionately more past than future. The New York chapter of the American Institute of Architects' Design for Aging Committee routinely convenes to discuss accessibility, diversity, intergenerational living arrangements, and transportation as strategies that can foster a sense of community by combating isolation. In the *New York Times*, Joseph Lelyveld's 1986 dispatch from Copenhagen explored why *selvbestemmelse*, or "self-determination," defines Denmark's "advanced Danish thinking on the care of the aged." In the *Guardian*, Helen Russell's 2016 report from Aarhus explored how a lifetime of paying nearly 50 percent in income taxes all but guarantees reliable services and amenities for Danish seniors. "Taking care of the whole of society has long been part of the Scandinavian tradition, and as a small, wealthy nation," she notes, "Denmark has been able to make changes more easily than might be possible in other countries."

Money matters when it comes to providing social services for seniors. European countries with traditions of (and mechanisms for) social welfare programs enshrined by taxes and legislative commitments tend to score better on this count. According to the most recent data (2017) from the Organisation for Economic Co-operation and Development (OECD), the Netherlands spends 3.7 percent of its GDP on health and social long-term care through a combination of government and compulsory insurance schemes for its seniors, Norway 3.3 percent, Sweden 3.2 percent, Denmark 2.5 percent, and Finland 2.1 percent. (Other countries that sit at or above OECD's 1.7 percent average include Belgium, France, Japan, Switzerland, and Iceland.) For the top five countries alone, that is $74 billion in long-term care costs in 2017 dollars.

Third-age housing proponents in the UK, which spends only 1.2 percent of its GDP on its seniors, argue that there is a lot of catching up to do compared with other countries. At a 2016 meeting of New London Architecture, a frequent convener and events host on built-environment topics, participants concluded that while it might be too late to adequately address the "tidal wave" of housing needs, London must make a better effort to "appreciate the widespread benefits and more balanced communities that intergenerational housing can bring."

The UK's Office for National Statistics counts more than 11.9 million men and women aged sixty-five or older among the country's population, or nearly 17.9 percent of the total population, with 3.2 million of this group over the age of eighty. (For comparison, Americans age sixty-five or older make up about 15.2 percent of the total US population.) As a proportion of the total population, this seems like a reasonable number, but with a density of 275 Britons per square kilometer, the housing challenges become evident. (Again, for comparison, the overall density in the United States is sixty-five Americans per square kilometer, or ninety-four per square mile.)

"Housing Our Ageing Population Panel for Innovation" (HAPPI) was published by thirteen researchers convened by Lord Richard Best and coordinated by Pollard Thomas Edwards (PTE).

"The time has come for a national effort to build the homes that will meet our needs and aspirations as we all grow older," begins a watershed 2009 report published in the UK, whose authors recommended sweeping changes in the way the country planned for the housing needs of an unprecedented number of Britons aged sixty-five or older. "We should all plan ahead positively, creating demand for better choice through a greater range of housing opportunities. Housing for older people should become an exemplar for mainstream housing, and meet higher design standards for space and quality."

The report, "Housing Our Ageing Population Panel for Innovation" (HAPPI), was published by thirteen researchers convened by Lord Richard Best, a former director of the British Churches Housing Trust, the National Housing Federation, and Joseph Rowntree Housing Trust. Best and his colleagues commissioned Pollard Thomas Edwards (PTE) and Levitt Bernstein Associates (LBA) to survey twenty-four projects in the UK and Europe and highlight six case studies that could drive what they called a "national priority" to provide alternative housing options that appealed to older Britons who might be disadvantaged by staying in their existing homes. Moving older Britons out of their terraced houses, their two-up-two-down row houses, their cottages, and their flats had another advantage from a national perspective: ameliorating a housing crisis. By encouraging seniors to move to spaces that could better accommodate their needs, including their social well-being, the real estate market would soften somewhat at a time when many Britons, old and young, find themselves outpriced.

In its account of their HAPPI report participation, London-based PTE emphasizes the need for choice and community in making the case to move. PTE's third-age residential projects are typically designed around social hubs, "which provides facilities to support a range of activities," according to the report, and, in the planning stages, PTE employs textbook cohousing strategies to facilitate participatory design, develop shared expectations, and accommodate individual needs.

Today, the design considerations espoused by the report's authors seem sensible and even commonplace, but at the time, they were an important extension of burgeoning notions of salutogenic design (focused on holistic and preventative health rather than on solving problems created by disease) at the intersection of public health and private well-being. Flexible spaces suited to a range of mobility and health circumstances; unfettered natural daylight and lots of plant life indoors and outdoors; numerous energy efficiencies and sustainable principles throughout; and an emphasis on "shared facilities and hubs" as well as "external shared surfaces and home zones"— all design elements aimed at transforming the conversation about senior housing.

"These things guide our practice for third-age housing, which is always about balancing sociability and privacy, as well as daylight and nature. Those are the important things," says Patrick Devlin, a partner at PTE and chief coordinator of the HAPPI report. "One of the strands of the HAPPI report is that if you build things well with thoughtful designs, it's where people will want to live. We didn't foresee COVID ten years ago, naturally, but it has made people a bit more receptive to the ideas about community in one's third age and, really, at any time of life."

NEW GROUND COHOUSING, LONDON

The HAPPI report has been augmented and updated several times as the aging population has, indeed, become a national priority—a product of the report's reception and the severity of the housing crisis. Soon after its original publication, the National Design Awards (promoted by all the major professional associations of the UK, including the Royal Institute of British Architects) had also begun soliciting projects for a special HAPPI category in its annual awards, recognizing designs that demonstrated what "planning ahead positively" meant. In 2016, the HAPPI category featured its first cohousing winner, New Ground Cohousing, owned by the Hanover Housing Association and the Older Women's Co-Housing group (OWCH), and designed in collaboration with PTE's Patrick Devlin.

The OWCH was established more than twenty years ago by women interested in creating a bricks-and-mortar expression of their community and shared desire to be independent in their third age, golden years, or the period generally defined as ages sixty to eighty. They envisioned a development that was modest in size, with individual homes and the opportunity to share amenities, meals, and gardens. Working with the local association and charity Housing for Women, the OWCH community sought to create an affordable housing

New Ground was designed by PTE as third-age housing, a term that eschews the expectations of "retirement" and the assumptions of "senior" to posit a more inclusive phase of life.

development that fell squarely in the realm of alternative cohousing. The group found a good partner with PTE, established nearly half a century ago, which has a strong portfolio of cooperative developments, collectives, and cohousing communities that are founded on rigorous and inclusive resident engagement in the discovery and design processes.

The not-for-profit Hanover Housing (also involved in the HAPPI report) identified a site that formerly housed St. Martha's Convent Junior School, which operated from 1953 to 2009. PTE conducted four workshops with OWCH members to, at first, discuss mood boards full of symbols, words, and photographs of admired buildings, and later to discuss attitudes about privacy versus community, accessibility, and materiality. The fourth and final workshop centered on a critique of PTE's design proposal, ruling out unworkable solutions, like pie-shaped units in a single curving building, and deciding on how the interior garden and green would work.

Part of PTE's remit was a contextual approach to both the streetscape and the overall village scale of the neighborhood. New Ground's suburban setting in Barnet, a northern borough of London just inside the M25 motorway, makes it convenient to amenities, not to mention the somewhat less polluted climes of higher ground—at 427 feet above sea level, Barnet is one of the highest suburbs of London. The project is less than a two-minute walk from a tube station and less than a ten-minute walk from a bus station. Various banks and shops, a Boots Pharmacy, a Costa Coffee, the local history museum, and a village green adjacent to a parish church are all within

The Older Women's Co-Housing Group (OWCH) was established more than twenty years ago by women interested in creating a brick-and-mortar expression of their community and shared desire to be independent during their third age.

spitting distance—many of the hallmarks of convenience and gentility.

In 2016 and 2017, New Ground received multiple awards from the *Evening Standard*, European Collaborative Housing, and the *Sunday Times*, among other grantees. By all accounts, it has been a success story, with committed and happy residents, who live in twenty-five homes adjacent to a central common house, as well as communal planting plots and a greenhouse.

The overall interiority of the scheme for New Ground as a place apart from the outside world puts it squarely in the canon of cohousing projects developed over the last twenty years based on Danish precepts of balancing privacy and community. In plan, New Ground is an *L*, with frontage on a residential street of modest one- and two-story houses and an entrance at the crook of the *L*, which opens up to a generous interblock lawn and connects to a convenient parking court. From the street, the facade reads as a familiar sand-colored terrace house with a character that owes more to Adolf Loos than to nationwide homebuilder Taylor Wimpey. From the inner lawn looking back at the inside of the *L*, the project reads more like a reclaimed factory, with each section of its solar-panel-covered, sawtooth roof delineating a separate unit below.

Residents enjoy "progressive privacy," a term of art that cohousing residents celebrate as a way to have spaces of semi-public conviviality in literal balance with space of entirely private solitude. Devlin, the project architect for New Ground, says that the firm's original proposal called for a glazed wall in

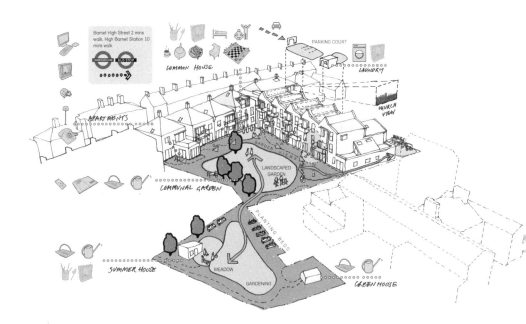

New Ground's suburban setting in Barnet, a northern borough
of London just inside the M25 motorway, makes it convenient to
amenities. Various banks and shops, pharmacy, coffee shop,
the local history museum, and a village green headed by a church
are nearby. In plan, New Ground is an L with frontage on a residential
street of modest one- and two-story houses and an entrance at the
crook of the L, which opens to a generous interblock lawn and
connects to a parking court.

the lobby, but this element was reduced to a small window in the group's design workshops. Today, residents can come and go relatively discreetly, or they may engage with lobby denizens. In contrast, most residents prefer to leave open the line of sight from their front windows to their back windows, even if they have installed a blind to interrupt that view. Progressive privacy allows them to choose for themselves where the balance is between community and privacy, mirroring the decisions we all make, consciously or unconsciously.

"To make these places successful, these residents have had to think through all of their boundaries and ideals and aspirations," says Devlin. "I think that's why they're so principled as people. Interdependence requires it. What's fascinating is that cohousing makes all of that explicit. It is honest about how we all live."

It is also emblematic of an honest approach to how architect-led design happens. One of the misperceptions of cohousing is that it is an unsavory line of work for architects looking to avoid the ruminations of a committee of clients. In truth, and according to nearly every source interviewed for this book, the architects held the pencils, so to speak, but the client group's best interests were matters of agreement and transparency.

In a 2015 article for the journal *Working with Older People*, Devlin and his coauthors from the OWCH and PTE put it this way: "PTE had declared from the beginning that the intention was not the near-impossible task of producing a development coherently designed by committee. Rather it was to help the group utilize their collective talents and experience to become an unusually well-informed client."

With only twenty-five units, New Ground has not made a significant dent in the UK's housing crisis, and the members of the OWCH were luckier than most to secure two adjacent and disused sites in a lovely and amenity-rich area of London, but the project does serve as a replicable model of cohousing for seniors.

"A lot of housing is badly designed and not great for the people who live in it—either physically or socially—and mainstream housing is not universally very good. New Ground's housing association saw cohousing as a way to figure out what people want. And, when you give people a choice, they make choices," says Devlin. "The main driver for third-age housing is the reality that, before COVID, you've got a lot of people who spend massively longer and more hours per day in their homes. After COVID, now we all spend more time in our homes. I'm not saying we got it all right with New Ground or the HAPPI report, but it turns out that the lessons of quality of life for older people's homes are important for everyone."

VILLAGE HEARTH, DURHAM, NORTH CAROLINA

COVID-19 has transformed everyday life in third-age housing in the UK and senior communities in the United States alike. Restricting the movements of visitors, implementing highly choreographed circulation patterns, addressing an unquenchable need for sanitizers and cleaning solutions, and paying urgent attention to air-circulation systems have

Village Hearth includes twenty-eight one-story cottages across seven buildings, each with its own backyard and front porch, connected by paths. The architecture of the cottages would be at home stylistically anywhere along the coast of the Southeast US from the Carolinas down to Key West.

busted institutional budgets and tested the mettle of both residents and their attending health care workers alike. But telehealth and interactive robots that will literally talk to you have helped keep residents connected. Agencies like the Centers for Disease Control, membership groups like the American Institute of Architects, and large architecture firms with thriving senior care studios or research initiatives like SmithGroup and Gensler have all issued recommendations for design improvements, systems upgrades, and social practices that can work in tandem to limit infections. Nonetheless, reports like the Kaiser Family Foundation's "Overlooked and Undercounted," published in September 2020, outline troubling gaps in accounting for both infection and death among residents and workers in senior communities. "Despite intense scrutiny of the number of COVID-19 cases and deaths in nursing facility settings, less than half of all states are reporting data for COVID-19 in assisted living facilities specifically," writes Sara True and her coauthors. "As a result," they continue, "it is difficult to know the extent to which residents and staff in assisted living facilities have been affected by COVID-19 or the extent to which interventions are urgently needed."

The reality of COVID-19's impact varies across the spectrum of senior communities, from nursing homes, memory care facilities, and assisted living facilities to independent living and "55 or better" active communities. But one impact is clear: pandemic-related isolation plays a part in the lives of everyone along this spectrum. Seniors facing fewer liberties thanks to COVID-19 and unable to participate in life

Founded by Pat McAulay and Margaret Roesch, Village Hearth claims
to be the first fifty-five-plus cohousing community in the United States
created by and for LGBTQ+ residents and their allies.

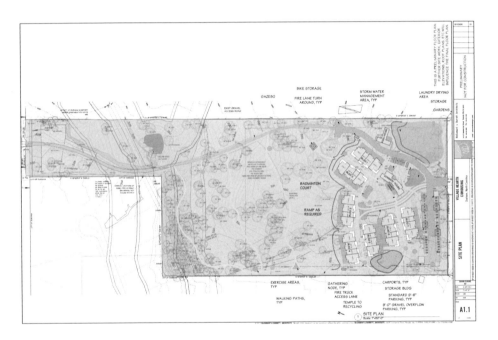

The site plan of Village Hearth demonstrates pedestrian-friendly walkability, within which the parking lot forms a spine along the site's south side that opens onto a series of connected paths encircling a common green area.

outside their brick-and-mortar communities have been resilient in redefining social capital, according to University of Pennsylvania Senior Fellow Carolyn Christa Cannuscio, who argues that social capital defines "successful aging" and is conferred on members of a community by virtue of their participation in that community—forming a reflexive system of action and identity that stands apart from social networks of people who simply know each other.

Indeed, an outcome of COVID-19 has also been the rising value of social capital among seniors, particularly in senior cohousing communities. "I would rather be here during COVID than anywhere else. Everyone is much more isolated out in the world than we are," says Dona McNeill, a resident of Village Hearth, which opened its doors only a couple of months before the COVID-19 outbreak. "We've made it our business to interact with each other safely. Because of COVID, we've bonded faster, in a sense."

Founded by Pat McAulay and Margaret Roesch, Village Hearth claims to be the first fifty-five-plus cohousing development in the United States created by and for the LGBTQ community. It includes clusters of twenty-eight one-story cottages across seven buildings, each with their own backyard and front porch, and each conceived by McCamant & Durrett Architects using "universal design" principles pioneered by the architect Ron Mace at North Carolina State University in 1989. In practice, Charles Durrett translated those principles to wide doors and roll-in showers to accommodate wheelchairs, low- or no-thresholds between spaces to support mobility, and low countertops to accommodate a range of circumstances. Village Hearth's common house contains all of the usual amenities found in cohousing common houses, such as a multipurpose room, a library, and an exercise room, and the entire project sits on five acres with ADA-compliant grading overlooking an additional ten acres of alders, dogwoods, and willows.

The site plan of Village Hearth demonstrates pedestrian-friendly walkability. The parking lot forms a spine along the site's south side and connects to a series of paths that encircle a common green area. Some paths lead to the common house while others terminate in a cul-de-sac. Each path is lined by connected, shiplap-clad cottages that would be at home architecturally anywhere along the southeast coast from the Carolinas down to Key West. Each home employs one of three different floor plans offering one- and two-bedroom configurations at three price points.

"One thing I liked in the workshops with Chuck [Durrett] is that he was not just helping us and guiding us through decisions about physical spaces, but he was teaching us about what it means to live as a community," says Linda Hobbet, who was among the first residents of Village Hearth, which broke ground in October 2018. "What attracted me to the concept was knowing your neighbors, mutual support, and working together. It wasn't so much about shared resources, although that's important, but about a growth opportunity. Staying engaged. Being active. Learning new things, and having lots of personal contact with people."

Durrett agrees that the design elements, as important as they are to the exigencies of everyday life, have little intrinsic value to a cohousing community without a strong pre-design workshop process. "I've done a lot of senior housing of all kinds, and seniors are resourceful, especially ones who design their own housing. They're naturally independent and opinionated people, and so the social side of the question is at least half of the solution," he says. "The buildings are just the frame. The people are the picture."

Hobbet and McNeill's neighbor, Jane Parrish, says that the "people" part stays in the picture, even after the community has been built. She reports that they are experimenting with a sociocracy governance model adapted to suit their goals, debating the annual homeowners-association budget, and planning a proposed dog park. "One of the goals of consensus is allowing everyone to have a voice. It doesn't mean we totally agree, but it means we all have a say and we can decide on what's safe enough for now and good enough to try," she says. "We do things in rounds and bring everything to the community."

Two of Durrett's other recent senior cohousing projects, developed with Kathryn McCamant—Silver Sage Village (2007) in Boulder, Colorado, and Quimper Village (2017) in Port Townsend, Washington—have also benefited from the workshop-driven process of design and development. Besides what Durrett calls the near-impossible challenge of design by committee, another common misconception about cohousing workshops is that they represent charrettes that culminate in

At Silver Sage in Colorado, as with other cohousing communities, even if the architecture seems incidental to the community's dialogue, it embodies the community itself (not to mention its legal structure, ownership model, and resident ethos).

a design. It is true that they will end in a work of architecture, but the workshops are actually designed to adapt sociocracy principles, a spirit of consent, and even nonviolent communication tenets to produce an efficient and respectful dialogue. Even if the architecture seems incidental to the community's dialogue, it ultimately ends up embodying the community itself (not to mention its legal structure, ownership model, and resident ethos, whether it is active seniors or vegan eco-villagers). The architecture also symbolizes the community, long after its first residents move in, for prospective residents who must visualize the changes they think they want to make in their lives to join a cohousing community at any age of life.

One resident of Silver Sage who moved in long after it had opened (and was not part of the original group to participate in the workshops) describes her skepticism in ways that seem to resonate across the cohousing world. "We started out with a lot of reservations about cohousing in general and elder cohousing in particular. We didn't want endless meetings. We weren't at all sure how we felt about having other people around all the time since we were both more or less introverts," said Silvine Marbury Farnell in a 2005 compendium of interviews edited by David Wann, himself a resident of Harmony Village Cohousing in Colorado. "[But] many of the people who move into cohousing are introverts, too."

Farnell's comments represent a broader shift in expectations about aging. Bill Thomas, a geriatrician and senior advocate who is founder of the Green House Project and changingaging.org, insists that while the fact that we age cannot be changed, the conceptions around aging can. He is often cited by architects who specialize in senior housing as well as proponents of cohousing. Thomas is arguably the most vociferous voice on the related topics of choice and liberty in defining a dignified concept of aging.

Recently, he has focused his message on transforming the spreadsheets and profit margins that result in "big box" senior living communities, and his ideas have resonated with senior cohousing's architects who have long advocated for modest one- and two-story projects conceived through consensus and designed to balance independence and interdependence. In 2019, Thomas launched Minka, a company based in Ithaca, New York, that makes small, modular and prefabricated homes that are preloaded with the kinds of technologies that older adults find useful, like voice-activated systems. The company's marketing materials boast that "Minka takes a 'goldilocks' approach to housing; developing efficient, affordable compact homes that are not too big, and not too small." Thomas and his company's investors, the Covia Group and Ziegler Linkage Funds, are testing the concept in California, known for its labyrinthine building codes. The idea is if it can work there, it can work anywhere, and if successful, the company's goal to scale-down senior living in an environmentally friendly and affordable way could presumably work in any community.

"I honestly think that the leisure lifestyle vision of senior housing is perhaps going to be eclipsed by a vision of a kind of housing that keeps you happy, healthy, and well," said Thomas

Quimper Village residents in Washington benefited from the workshop- and consensus-driven process practiced by McCamant & Durrett and other cohousing architects.

in a Senior Housing News podcast in March 2020. "Rather than a lifestyle, aspirational retirement lifestyle, it's going to refocus the value proposition for senior housing around some core variables having to do with health and wellness."

In something of a coda to Thomas's words, the wellness industry led by wellness influencers was thrust into the limelight in 2020. Even if the roots of wellness as a term extend to alternative medicines of the 1970s (and well-being as a term as far back to the World Health Organization's constitution first published in 1948), the notion that health isn't just the opposite of illness has been widely accepted by a broader cross-section of the population thanks to the issues raised by COVID. In an August 2020 op-ed in the *New York Times*, Amanda Hess chronicled how wellness was being peddled by celebrities who felt "empowered to recast their quarantine as a self-actualization incubator." On the campaign trail and after his November 2020 election win, President Joe Biden spoke of wellness as a principle of health-care reform and a common-sense rationale for vaccine mandates. Preventative medicine and lifestyle changes have also been bundled by corporate human resource programs at Fortune 500 companies under the banner of wellness (thereby helping those companies realize insurance-premium savings).

But, just as the term *senior living* does a poor job of conveying how many different types of group living arrangements are available to seniors today, the term *wellness* does an equally poor job of conveying that our quest to live well depends on how well we live among others. Statistics about loneliness among seniors aside, people who study group dynamics and individual wellness point to a vital balance between who we associate with and why we can't do it alone. A pandemic solved through virology, vaccines, and social distancing doesn't prove this point so much as it reveals the proof that has existed all along: we all live together by design. Some people are just more inclined than most of us to engage the design process.

Acknowledgments

Jan Hartman had the good idea for a book about cohousing at a time when the movement had been active for many decades, but the subject had only started to gain ground in popular media as a worthwhile alternative to conventional ways of living. I am indebted to Jan as the book's first champion, commissioning editor, and enthusiastic advocate, and her perspective has been foundational to my thinking. I also want to thank Lynn Grady, Abby Bussel, Michelle Meier, and the team at Princeton Architectural Press for their hard work to deliver this book to market. I am indebted to the architects and residents I interviewed for this book, whose experiences and impressions were essential to my understanding of cohousing and communal living. I am grateful to William Morgan, who lent a critical ear throughout the research and writing of this book and suggested a project in Maine that proved fascinating. Evelyn Staudinger and Tripp Evans offered me the valuable opportunity to test some of the ideas in this book by inviting me to deliver the Heuser Lecture at my alma mater, Wheaton College, for which I am grateful. I am also indebted to Françoise and Thomas Vonier for their hospitality in offering me space to work during my writing jags and in feeding me. Finally, I must thank my wife and partner, Pascale Vonier, for her patience and support from beginning to end. This project could not have been completed without her help.

Further Reading

This book benefited from unpublished interviews conducted by the author with cohousing architects and residents. For further reading, here is a list of secondary sources that reflect the breadth of approaches scholars and journalists have taken to chronicle trends in cohousing, communal living, and intentional living. It is by no means exhaustive.

Barac, Matthew, Julia Park, and Patrick Devlin. *Housing Our Ageing Population: Panel for Innovation*. London: Homes and Communities Agency, 2009.

Boyer, Robert H. W. and Suzanne Leland. "Cohousing for Whom? Survey Evidence to Support the Diffusion of Socially and Spatially Integrated Housing in the United States." *Housing Policy Debate* 28, no. 5, (2018): 653–667.

Chatterton, Paul. "Towards an Agenda for Post-Carbon Cities: Lessons from Lilac, the UK's First Ecological, Affordable Cohousing Community." *International Journal of Urban and Regional Research* 37, no. 5 (2013): 1654–74.

Christian, Diana Leafe. *Creating a Life Together: Practical Tools to Grow Ecovillages and Intentional Communities*. Gabriola Island, British Columbia: New Society Publishers, 2003.

Crawford, Sheri F. "Arcosanti: An American Community Looking Toward the Millennium." *Communal Societies: Journal of the Communal Studies Association* 14 (1994): 49–66.

Durrett, Charles. *Senior Cohousing: A Community Approach to Independent Living*. 2nd edition. Gabriola Island, British Columbia: New Society Publishers, 2009.

Hanson, Chris and Chris ScottHanson. *The Cohousing Handbook: Building a Place for Community*. Vancouver: Hartley & Marks Publishers, 1996.

Ferrara, Mark S. *American Community: Radical Experiments in Intentional Living*. New Brunswick, NJ: Rutgers University Press, 2020.

Festinger, Leon. "Architecture and Group Membership." *Journal of Social Issues* 7, nos. 1–2 (1951): 152–63.

Fromm, Dorit, "American Cohousing: The First Five Years." *Journal of Architectural and Planning Research* 17, no. 2 (Summer 2000): 94–109.

Gutman, Robert. "The Questions Architects Ask." *Transactions of the Bartlett Society, Bartlett School of Architecture, University College, London* 4 (1965–1966): 49–82.

Larsen, Henrik Gutzon. "Three Phases of Danish Cohousing: Tenure and the Development of an Alternative Housing Form." *Housing Studies* 34, no. 8 (2019): 1349–71.

Levitt, Alexandria and Charles Durrett. *State-of-the-Art Cohousing: Lessons Learned from Quimper Village.* Self-published, Kindle Direct Publishing, 2020.

Martin, Courtney. "Modern Housing with Village Virtues." *New York Times,* September 20, 2016. https://www.nytimes.com/2016/09/20/opinion/modern-housing-with-village-virtues.html.

McCamant, Kathryn and Charles Durrett. *Cohousing: A Contemporary Approach to Housing Ourselves.* 2nd edition. Berkeley, CA: Ten Speed Press, 1994.

Pedersen, Max. "Senior Co-Housing Communities in Denmark." *Journal of Housing For the Elderly* 29, nos. 1–2 (2015): 126–45.

Wann, David, ed. *Reinventing Community: Stories from the Walkways of Cohousing*. Golden, CO: Fulcrum Publishing, 2005.

Williams, Gisela. "The Fancy Neighborhood of the Future Is an Earth-Friendly 'Intentional Community.'" Bloomberg. com, April 6, 2020. https://www.bloomberg.com/ news/features/2020-04-16/earth-friendly-intentional -communities-are-new-fancy-neighborhood.

Williams, Jo. "Designing Neighbourhoods for Social Interaction: The Case of Cohousing." *Journal of Urban Design* 10, no. 2 (2005): 195–227.